MIRAGES

Issa Makhlouf

Mirages

Translated by Alicia F. Lam

The Post-Apollo Press

Library of Congress Cataloging-in-Publication Data

Makhlouf, Issa.
[Poems. Selections. English]
Mirages / Issa Makhlouf ; translated by Alicia F. Lam ; originally written in Arabic and translated into French by Nabil El Azan.
pages cm
ISBN 978-0-942996-85-2 (alk. paper)
I. Lam, Alicia F., translator. II. El Azan, Nabil, translator. III. Title.
PJ7846.A4947A2 2015
892.7'16--dc23
2015018999

The Post-Apollo Press
35 Marie Street
Sausalito, California 94965
www.postapollopress.com

Book Design by Simone Fattal
Cover drawing by Etel Adnan
Typeset by Lindsey Boldt in Hoefler text
with Minion Pro for display

Printed in The United States on acid-free paper

Contents

♦ ♦ ♦

What I tell today are stories that I waited to hear from someone.
What I tell is only a part of what I have not seen.
Had I seen, I wouldn't have told.

We Leave

We leave to distance ourselves from our birthplace and to see the other side of dawn. We leave to look for our improbable births. To complete our alphabets. To load our farewell with promises. To go as far away as the horizon, tearing apart our destinies and scattering their pages before finding, sometimes, our own life story in other books.

We leave to unknown destinies. To tell those we have met that we will return to resume our relationship. We leave to learn the language of the trees which never leave. To polish the jingling bells in the sacred valleys. To search for more merciful gods. To remove the mask of exile from foreigners. To confide to passers-by that, like them, we are also passers-by, and that our permanence in memory and oblivion is ephemeral, far away from mothers who light candles of absence and shorten the span of time every time they raise their hands to heaven.

We leave to avoid seeing our parents grow old, to avoid reading their days on their faces. We leave in anticipation of distracted and wasted lives. We leave to reassure those whom we love that we will always love them, that our admiration is stronger than distance, and that exile can be as sweet and fresh as our own homeland. We leave so that, when we return home one day, we will realize that we are bound to be exiles wherever we are.

We leave to eliminate the difference between air and air, water and water, heaven and hell. Making fun of Time, we contemplate the immensity of space. In front of us, the waves jump like children, while the sea flows between two ships. One of them departs and the other, made of paper, is held in the hands of a child.

We leave like the clown who moves from village to village with his animals, teaching children their first lesson in boredom. We leave to deceive death, letting it follow us from place to place. We continue to leave until we are lost, until we can no longer find ourselves in the places we went, until we are lost and no one can find us anymore.

- I -

The Rain Burns

Near the Morning Bread

The evening breeze brings Sappho's voice to me. It brings me the sacred geometry of her voice, a dream that emerges at the edge of night, which I can see from my balcony, through a fine rain dissipating in the mist.

How can we touch her light amid the brightness of a sun that is setting before her astonished eyes? All the promises of eternal life, all the gardens of Eden dreamed in her voice are for him, for the man who has in his heart a little bit of her. A little bit of hope.

Hope is unique and undivided. The tree of hope is unique too. They are a lure invented against the truth of everyone's despair. The tree of hope emerges only in distant places. As revenge, the seed of desperation, which is poisonous, germinates everywhere. Inside the body as well as out. It is part of pedestrian feelings. Hatred, resentment, hypocrisy, jealousy. It is also hunger, cold, humiliation, and thirst. It is a desire for war and a rain of ashes over Hiroshima, and from then on, a rain over the whole world. Black rain that keeps falling, splashing the spirit with indelible stains. Lack of love.

Oh Sappho, what can we do to create a love free of life or death? Love that doesn't hide its sharp blade under its open wings amid the nakedness of time. I hear you say that man's time has not yet come! Then, when and how will it come?

The evening breeze brings your voice to me. Two thousand six hundred years after its first eruption, there, very near the streams of Greek tragedy and the myths where men and gods fought one another. You murmur:

> A woman's body after making love.
> The corpse waiting for us to cover it with oblivion.
> Oblique fall.

The fall of the bodies that we love, one after another.
The measures of the fall: the ruler and the square.
The geometry of destruction.
The immense destruction that couldn't be conceived without an
    immense geometrical design.
The destruction of the temple as the destruction of the ritual...

You ask whether there is still love. A little bit of love among men. Among men and beasts. Among beasts and plants. Or whether we have started a new war that renders the old weapons obsolete.

You ask whether people still open mythology books and remove the ashes of the dead to look for fire. Or whether death is dead. And whether the nostalgia for the dead, which sometimes visits us in our dreams, has been exhausted. The dead who we love, who we wish to see again respond to our call without delay. They wait for us on the other shore where they welcome us to the border of dreams. Without daring to come too near, afraid the boundary may break.

I repeat this word incessantly, your word, until I make it mine. We leave ourselves like one who abandons a house in which he no longer wants to reside. Where did everyone who used to live there go, shuddering in the air, trembling behind the windows, roaring with laughter, perfuming our hearts? Where did those who allowed us to look for a color to paint boredom and a word to designate the eternal coldness of the churches in Europe go? Wherever we are today, we no longer know whether the path to choose is ahead or behind us. Where is the path and in which direction should we step?

No, it is not the golden rain falling on Danaë either. On her body as it writhes in pain. Behind the curtain that separates us, I hear her sighing as she says, "How can we end time without ending life? And if we cannot end it, what will we do?"

Will it be necessary to build a world without ruins and memories? We approach simple things, with no goal or objective. Like the brightness of the moon that tames the mountains, inviting it to sit on terraces with us. A meeting in which you'll be absent once again. In front of your house an infinite greenness extends itself.

There are voices that are replaced by music. The first of the *Duino Elegies* comes to mind. The eyes of the small animal that kept me company for a month during my childhood. The seas that remained a promise in books. The strong wind that blew above those seas, making the waves roar like the womb of a nine-month-pregnant woman, blew inside my head. No, I haven't traveled yet, but I dream of it endlessly.

We haven't seen our faces reflected on the water. The stained glass thrown into the sea comes from Venice, from the time the Grand Canal was ablaze along with the glass, a mirror, a golden ring, and a braid of your hair. These vestiges are there, near the Accademia where Bellini's Madonna—the most beautiful woman in Italy stands.

On the way back, we will go to the place we used to go. We will go up, facing the rays of the setting sun, busily transplanting the cypresses somewhere else. There, we will forget about everything happening around us, or pretend to do so. Oh you, little bird hidden in the shade of leaves and branches, I no longer know whether you are hiding or dying.

The evening breeze brings Sappho's voice to me, radiant, powerful like mountain sun after rain. Faithful mountains who cast anchors into the land, right here, very near the morning bread.

In the Dark Bedroom

In the dark bedroom, light doesn't come in from a window or a slit in the wall, but from the fusion of gums and the separation of two lips full of happiness.

No one can possess anyone or anything. No one can possess even the self. What does the river that flows out possess? What does the shining star possess? What about the sun that spits its volcanoes? And the silent upright tree, unchanging in appearance? The great silence itself, so propitious to build its home...

One stands in front of a mirror, but there's no one in the mirror. Whoever has lost his sight knows that: what can be seen is just a small part of what is visible. What can be seen hides something else, invisible at first sight. Just invisible. Can feelings be seen? What about the populated air? And the vast plains and the flock of birds always taking off? It's the desire to know who makes of earth a big waiting room for the afterlife. Or rather, the part of earth that is imperceptible.

Is the bedroom still dark even though one is not alone? Even though the world is crowded and its inhabitants are squashed together in balconies without railings? I observe your naked breasts through the semidarkness of the mirror. Is it true that what can be seen is only part of what is visible? I observe the child who will be born from your round womb, a majestic mountain. Mountains that can be replaced by poems become inaccessible. If we can observe them, why write about them? To contemplate these moving sculptures, day after day. We touch them and are blessed by them. The solitary tree is my canopy. A tree that grows out of the earth and sky.

Does the bedroom remain dark after lips—your lips—separate? And this light, where does it come from? It's on the canvases of Caravaggio or

Rembrandt, and in those tombs made of marble for the exclusive use of queens of death. From the Taj Mahal, whose white marble is consumed by time, to gardens of jasmine. From the pink palaces of Petra to the stained glass windows of churches. And from the Alhambra in Granada to the tiny palace of Amra in Jordan, with its baths, colored murals of women, and the voice of buried water. Whose hands sculpted your light in the darkness? And why does it stay in that great hall, under a canopy? There, death embraces us, but we don't die. Affectionately, we pamper each other, reinventing our mornings in the deepest crack of the disintegrating night.

Does darkness remain dark when the body revolts against its shroud? The body tears its shroud and goes back to huddle in the woman's womb. The first womb that opens up for it. It is the very first moment of a genesis greater than the universe. It is outside both the mirror and the canopy at once. Far away from what calls the spirit a spirit and the body a body.

What happens to darkness when you pull down the curtains and walk white and barefoot in the locked bedroom? You touch the smooth surface and your foam spreads over the body lain before you. Haven't you seen the vain foam of fountains? Deviating from its old paths, it ascends with the spirit's wakefulness. It is precisely the heat of the darkness' foam that reaches me, but I can't reach it. Those pearls of yours, viscous and black. The soft metal yawning in your entrails.

Work begins through the cracks of the night. The woman closes her eyelids and lips again over yet a greater mystery. She learned to listen to the murmur of her baby so well that now she lies in wait for the least of warning signs. Later, when milk bursts out of her breasts, responding to the call of hunger, she will think of the springs buried in the darkness of the earth, next to the pulsating heart of its volcanoes. There, where darkness never precedes light, nor follows it.

In the dark bedroom, you sit next to me and turn to me to speak. You still speak in my mouth. And every time I brush against your whisper, a

cloud starts to swirl above the mountains. I name you the unnamable. You repeat the same word incessantly.
"Lying," you say. "The sharing of the lie."

What can a tattered language—an instrument no longer good for laughing or crying—say? What can we say when words freeze between our lungs?

I stand still in front of the stained glass window. Panting, I pass my index finger on the exhaled mist. There, I draw a line that goes nowhere.

The Dream

Once again, the dream comes to me. That dream where we cross the Court Carrée of the Louvre together, before exiting through the gate that leads to the main street. The old church of meticulously carved stones appears before us. There, light and shadow play in every corner. In front of the church there is a great carriage full of bells. Where did those bells come from? Some big, others small, around which people now gather. We join them as if summoned. Like them, we wait under the light rain, to see what will happen, without being certain that anything will happen at all. There is a secret need, among all the people gathered here, for something to happen. Something unforeseen, something unexpected. And these bells—around twenty of them!—piled up inside the carriage. Perhaps the church is emptying itself of its celestial burden? And which unknown monks brought them here, abandoning then before the great door like we abandon unwanted newborns on the steps of orphanages? We wait a long time. Then, as we are about to leave, we look at all the faces watching, eyes fixed on the bells as if ordering them to speak. All at once, mechanically, the bells begin and it's as if we have never heard ringing before.

Where is the electrical switch capable of turning them on, and whose finger flipped it? We don't move from our place until the end. It happens all at once, like in the beginning of this story, leaving us with a great emptiness. Turning our backs to the bells, we enter the church. It is all in shadow, except for one corner, illuminated by altar candles. Like two butterflies, we move toward the flames intensifying the darkness around them.

I have never had a dream like this before. Standing side by side, we silently watch the smoke rise before us. Then, we approach the candles, light one together, and before placing it back among the others. "Let's each make a wish," you say, closing your eye lids for a few moments, as if assuring yourself that from now on you will keep your wish engraved inside you forever. You don't wait long to reopen them, revealing shining eyes. They are so pure in the incandescent glow of the candles that I perceive a tear held back by your eye, intensifying your beauty. But I realize suddenly that you are nude and am surprised I didn't notice earlier. You are completely naked. It isn't this nudity that I desire in you, but another kind of nudity I ignore. A strange and painful nudity. You are naked like the body of Christ. Wounded and abandoned before eyes that look with a final piercing blow. And that smile, that smile that lights up the darkness inscribes stigmata in the air.

Vision of the Sun

Beyond Sight

He was not born in the desert, nor in its surroundings. Yet, since his sweet childhood, he has dreamed of staying there to count the grains of sand, one by one. He was convinced that a treasure was buried there, and that the sand was a marvelous treasure trove.

He was not born in the East. Yet, he could hear it speak inside him. One day, he secretly entered his father's office. He found a book that he had never seen before. Wanting to leaf through it, particularly to read a passage from Ecclesiastes, he realized that this book hid another. Its title was One thousand and one nights. He read it and fell asleep. When he woke up, he found that he had lost his sight. He remembered that in his dream he had seen an Orient of aurora and gold.

Since then, he knows that everything around him is an illusion and the world is a labyrinth—whoever enters it is lost once and for all, just as one loses one's mind at the approach of an infinite memory that is unverifiable. And every morning, he is surprised to find that he is still himself. He is struck with boredom. He tells himself that life is nothing but a dream and that he doesn't fear death, but rather immortality. When he happened to write, it was only for himself, for some friends, and for the sake of lightening the weight of time.

A dignified member of a lineage of great blind writers across the ages, here he is, The Blind One, from Homer to Milton to Al-Ma`arri. And even though he was already living in the middle of an illuminated mist, he never took into account the Shakespearean expression: "Look into the darkness, where the blind can see."

The blind one says, "There is such solitude in that gold." Who says that the blind one can't see? He sees in his own way. He sees the loneliness of metal and its terrible isolation. Metal that is extracted from earth and rock, like an oyster is extracted from its shell, from the bottom of the sea. It's this solitude that uncovers the entrails of the earth and the movement of the universe. And this gold, is it the heart of the universe? Is it silent radiation turned to frost? Or is it a distant light that hasn't reach us yet? We, the infants of a forgotten earth.

And the blind one wonders, "Why do we see only with our eyes, those two sugary balls? Why not the whole body? Isn't it that the body is a transition to dust through the channels of doubt and certainty? Is it not the evanescent foam, falling vainly into its abyss?" Hardly has he formulated the question, when he is already sure that he can't be sure of anything.

His first piece of writing was a poem. That is, a simple attempt to comprehend the breath of time and to return to places forever lost. That's how he started to dream of distant cities that he would never be able to see because his blindness would cover them with his shadow. Of seas bitten by dolphin teeth which he would never sail. And of lodgings where he would spend one night, never two, to imagine a sea, a plain, or a mountain, and to listen to music, sometimes with the feeling that he was close to grasping something he would never be able to express. Because writing and labyrinth, writing and mirrors, mirrors and masks, night and compass, all these are just reflections of things, nothing more.

Convinced that we don't invent anything new, but rather repeat past inventions and entire destinies of writing, he enjoyed reading more than writing. Either by writing or narrating, he gave the impression that he was reciting texts he had already read; in other words, by writing them he did not write, he remembered. This is how he was allowed to attribute all the texts he wanted to himself. Why on earth would he rewrite texts that he would have liked to have authored? Surely, he was the author, but as if written by another hand. The hand of the other.

He observed the first letter of the alphabet for so long that he managed to see the sun. He tried to express this vision. So he wrote a poem that made no sense, like all great poems, because the poem that submerges itself in the mystery of the world intends to express nothing. There, the Aleph is the solar disc. A window over the infinite blueness. The window opens for Him. "He, as simple as the Aleph," according to the phrase by Rûmî. He, the multiple One, the Almighty. The One who neither rewards nor punishes. Yet, from afar, He watches His creatures. He observes them through a veil that does not hide His beauty or the gift of His light; on the contrary, it enhances His brightness. He does not distinguish among human, animal, and mineral. He contemplates them with the compassion of one who does not ignore their fatal ending. And with the certainty that if someday these creatures destroy themselves, an atom of dust would turn around itself and then become a blade of grass. The same thing would happen should the libraries of the world burn.

Knowing that the universe doesn't stop rotating around itself, and around the sun, he remembered the library of Alexandria. Thinking that the generations to come would rewrite all the masterpieces that were reduced to ashes, he dedicated one of his poems to the one who torched the library. Nothing gets lost in this world. Lost here, recovered there. Because resurrection is born from death, and blindness brings forth vision. And so, the blind one, who knows everything that sight embraces, also knows what is beyond sight. It is there where he lives.

Moreover, the blind one doesn't have to close his eyes in order to sleep. He is completely free between wakefulness and sleep, or between dream and reality. There are no doors or thresholds separating the two spaces. The doors are always open! This is how the blind one sees in secret. That is where he floats, like a cloud above the sand.

One day, when he was more than eighty years old, someone warned him, "You'll die tomorrow morning because you revealed the secret of the gods and you stole their sacred fire." On the next day, as he was crossing the street that separated his house from the public library, a thief—the great majority of his friends were such—approached him, stabbed him in his chest twice, and left.

The blind one knew beforehand that he wouldn't live long enough to see the most beautiful face, that which defies age, dazzling and pure, like the gold that comes before everything, including earth itself.

Groundwater

In the Lascaux Cave, next to a disemboweled bison lies the body of a man with a birdlike head. His sexual organ is erect. Next to the man, there is a stick crowned with a bird. This scene, painted by the hand of a man almost twenty-thousand years ago, is unique in its genre. Why should we suddenly speculate as the ritual sense disappears?

Succinct fine lines show man and animal with a precision that does not tolerate anything superfluous. There is a soberness that only deals with the essence. Farther away, near the edge of the painting that covers the whole rocky surface of the cave, a hand can be seen. Or perhaps it is the shadow of a hand emerging suddenly from the rock. Suddenly—twenty-thousand years later. The open hand is the same in all secular caves. This hand, open to the unknown, sifted by a red halo, is our bare hand symbolizing our path from beginning to end.

In the calm of the raised hand, indicating the restlessness of man and his fear of himself and the alien world that surrounds him, man and animal fraternize. All living beings with a common destiny fraternize. The hand is abandoned and covered with dust as time passes, carrying the message from the past to the future. And so, mystery besieges the open hand that is about to reunite with its first cloud. The more open it is, the more mysterious it becomes. As if death were the guardian of the boundary between the hand that paints and the hand that is painted above an eternal altar. The hand vanishes, the painting remains. Meanwhile, the cloud hides in a water spring that only those who are lost can find.

In a Lascaux night, which is our distant night, we see sex and death in harmony and agreement. We also see the first sign emerging through the darkness of the soul. We delve into our memory in vain. Ah, as if we had any memory! Did man have any actual memory before the invention of the computer? We secretly celebrate the answer before even formulating the question. What?! Should we suddenly ignore books? All those smooth colored pages, pressed, printed with letters, with spaces between two words, two paragraphs. Those pages are next to one another and they ebb and flow like sea waves.

Those books are like the ships we have boarded over the centuries, taking us into the depth of seas we would never have thought of reaching. And long before books, our primitive memory was engraved on surfaces made of brick, clay, skin, and papyrus. Mythical tales can be read there, as well as epic poems narrating the creation of the universe and the battles of destinies which describe how currents and blood flow, how fire burns and extinguishes inside a heart. This is the fire that writes us, but whose sense vanishes from us.

Today, going back to the mythical tales, we realize that the ancient gods who ruled the world in the past still live among us, wearing masks of different style and form. The two main gods were the god of love and the god of war. Man's fate on this planet is still in the hands of these two gods.

Twenty-thousand years ago. Twenty-thousand years ahead. From the depth of the earth, from the caves where it is always dark as in an eternal night, to the surface of the earth, and as far away as the borders of a wounded sky struck by a thousand arrows every instant. We are here, with our hand reaching out to the shooting star, indicating that time has come. The greatest hope comes from the greatest pain. A hand is extended to welcome us when we find ourselves in the depth of the abyss. This hand pours over our face what we need to bear sadness as well as happiness. Both feelings always come to us in the same astonishing chariot.

I watch the trees one by one. I watch the stones one by one. I watch them and I know that there is a long history between us, and that our return to groundwater is imminent.

Wounded by His Light

No look escapes the painting's frame. The characters seem pushed toward the body lying on the ground, dissolving into the landscape, huddled together in a moment of complete abandonment.

It is in the lower part of the painting where the limbs find their way, as if they were underwater or in the womb. They are arranged in evident sensuality. There is something in the smooth bodies of the women. Bodies without imperfection; a mixture of red, violet, and blue.

Among the women, he is the only one who is naked. The only one lying on the ground. Four women. The closest one to him, carries a torch, and kneels next to him. At her left there is another woman with open arms, and behind, the last two. One is wiping away her tears and the other is praying.

While the wound is in place, it holds. His right leg lifted in front of the slack left. The opening of the arms. The warmth of his naked chest. His head slightly elevated and falling backwards. The women to the right; his head back. Relaxed or languid? From left to right, they, the women, work their way up all the branches of his body.

In the painting, the spear's blow does not injure the body but decorates it. It leads the body beyond the duality of life and death, toward its splendor, in search of the light buried inside him, inaccessible beauty. Lying before you, he leaves the world and stays at the same time... You see him as if in a dream. A dream that nevertheless opens on wakefulness and flows. A dream that contains everything. Dream of full awakening in this scattered body.

What is the woman who carries the torch looking for in the extinguished face? What do her wide-open eyes expect to see? Who is the mother and who is the lover? How can one expression be distinguished from another in the light of this poor flame? While Teresa cries marble tears under Bernini's chisel, here, no one is crying. Everyone is silent over the face and body of Sebastian. All feelings are kept inside. Regrouped in heaven. I contemplate at length his distracted presence and I hear him say, "The one who removes the spear from my chest will kill me. Pierced, my life runs by my side like a river. Illuminate my face, oh, living torch! Let your secret infiltrate in the deepest part of the interstice between light and shadow, in ecstatic celebration of a trance, not of death."

The Trustworthy Man

He was obsessed with time, which he spoke of with a philosophical tone.

I never thought I would meet a philosophical thief one day. He used to say that prison was the ideal place to grow old. There, time deposits itself on a man like dregs in the bottom of a glass.

He used to say, "In prison, days pass by slowly and time is frozen; it doesn't flow."

♦♦♦

Sometimes I have the strange feeling that even if his hands were cut off he would continue to steal. He would steal with his elbows, feet, knees, or mouth. As long as the breath of life is in him, he will continue to steal, he knows that well. Guardian of a mystery that he doesn't understand himself.

The thief, do you know who he is?

This particular thief, not just any thief. I mean the one who secretly breaks into your house, steals a little money or some gold object to resell, and then comes back to you, gift in hand, another gold object, or a bouquet of flowers!

He mentioned once that he steals just for the sake of stealing. Victim of his mystery. Of this secret force that seeps into his hands, a force that drives him to the act. He just opens the door and slides behind the curtains.

This peculiarity, so natural and typical of him, beats forcefully inside his chest, pushing him to steal, like others are pushed to kill.

He knows beforehand that he will fall into the trap, and he won't be able to do anything to stop his own demise, like the seagull that crashes into the surface of the water with its eyes open in order to hunt, and then, because of the impact, loses its sight.

He confuses reality and fiction, and is astonished when he sees the blood of immaterial victims spurt.

♦♦♦

This particular thief has long tapered fingers, laden with rhythm and movements in agreement with the his facial expressions. Fingers that move without him when he speaks, chipping invisible cracks in the air. And fingers that abandon modesty when he doesn't speak.

It's with these hands, with these fingers that he steals. Two hands that appear, at first sight, devoted to generosity and grace. Two hands that tremble at the moment of theft, carrying away his entire being with them. As if he were the first one to feel fear, he, the thief. Robbed of himself, he is the first to be afraid of himself.

♦♦♦

Thief and lover. That's him.

He says, "How weak I am, soft and prone to fall as soon as the woman I love hurts me. Let me descend from your throne and strike me one fatal blow instead of all these benign blows."

Show me someone who is deprived of love and I will embrace him! That one is my brother.

THE GERANIUM'S FAREWELL

On that April morning, the movers arrived and carried everything away: the small bed, the TV set, the wardrobe, the kitchenware, the toiletries, the curtains, the library with all the books it contained: files, newspaper clippings, and family pictures...Carefully and methodically, the movers packed the objects from the apartment; each thing in its place. Everything made of glass in a box padded with a red cloth which, having its corners torn in places, let the plastic bubble wrap show through. The cutlery in a rough wooden chest without decoration, and the clothes in a large suitcase. Then, they brought everything down to load into the truck parked in front of the apartment. They carried away everything except the flowers lined up in a big rectangular flower box suspended over the black wrought iron handrail.

Nine geraniums decorated the flower box and lifted their heads toward the light, like the only witnesses of your coming and of your premature departure. In the interval, between your arrival and your departure, they have been your silent animals. They, who watched over your sleep, assisting the opening of your eyelids every morning. They and your our balcony overlooking a dawn that breaks somewhere you thought would be a happier place to live.

That short trip that preceded your final departure was decisive. Weeks after, these flowers remained as straight as they could, struggling not to fade, in spite of the rain which was, at that moment, scarce. When you came home, they rejoiced, believing you were home for good. But you did not hear the call of the buds growing among the nearly dead leaves.

Nine blood-red flowers have decorated your window for the past twelve months. Leaning on the wood of the black handrail. Accompanying your movements and the quivering of your muscles, one by one. Listening to you and watching for the silent chatter between the inside and the outside. Welcoming your tired gaze by dint of wandering in vague directions. Nine friends. Assuring yourself of their number every day. You watered them. Caressed by their stems and leaves. And, banished the dust with your breath.

Whenever you felt like reading aloud from striking passages in a book, it was, without knowing, for them that you did it too. When you hummed a tune you liked, they were the molecules pouring out all around you. At the hour when clouds covered the sky, spreading a veil over the city, you stared at them through the glass of the closed window, as if those red petals were the stars of your night. Those within reach, you would stroke at your leisure, asking them questions no one had yet dreamed of.

During the last weeks, you neglected them. Even worse, you completely forgot them. Like a storm, life came to tear you from yourself, cutting you off from your daily rituals. And the petals mixed with the dried flowers in the pot. And the buds, invaded by a mixture of yellowish green and pale brown leaves, withdrew.

Upon leaving the apartment that sunny morning, you threw one last look around to be sure that no trace of yourself was left behind, that the place stood completely empty, like the first day you came, but the nine plants didn't stop you. Had you stopped to look at them, the red that was left would have blinded you. As meager as it was, it shone in the sun. You shunned them. Weren't they shunned already? Plants are unlike us when it comes to waiting for the moment of a breakup to feel what there is to feel. It hits home instantly. With lightning quick intuition, they know that a breakup never occurs in a sudden way or with a single blow, but that it begins profoundly from the very first day...

Was forgetting the flowers merely an oversight? Or were you convinced that breakups only cause pain to humans and animals, not to plants? Like the broken man when he suddenly sees himself alone, isolated in a chimerical world?

Feeling of imminent drowning. There, where there's no more time for anything, even for what passes before our eyes, there are still some of the most beautiful moments, the most pure.

The Pregnant Woman

She is there, naked, standing in front of the same oblong mirror, facing herself in a moment charged with doubt, torment, and obscure light. She places her hands on her belly as if it were a small universe. She tries to surround it on all sides. Her hands seem longer than normal, as if they have elongated since her pregnancy. She approaches the mirror. Her belly grazes the cold, brilliant surface. But then, concerned for the fetus, she recoils. She fears that such contact may disturb it. That the external cold could seep inside. Where does he, who comes to the world through her, come from? She asks herself. Again, she approaches the mirror, stopping at a distance sufficient enough to distinguish the transformations her pregnancy has made on her face and body.

After laying colorful, shimmering sheets of delicate material on the floor, the pregnant woman lies down on her back. She raises her knees. Opens her legs wide, and looks in the mirror.The full and swollen lips move. Opening in a delicate, sensual smile, "Soft flesh opens for your arrival into the world."

As for him, this dream became a body, and if he stayed a secret in her heart? The shadow of her desire for him? A butterfly flying like the beating of a heart? And if he remained the fixed note of her whisper when she prayed in the evening? It surprises her then that she is in such disarray before dusk in the saturated calm of departure. A departure without regret or sorrow, because this separation is as light as the shadow of a giant tree on the shoulder of a child. The world is light. And the earth is light, turning around until forming an eclipse.

Can the woman come out of isolation by giving birth? Can she become two at once? Can she acquire that full self, crowned with a halo of incomparable radiance? Or would the woman, or more exactly her body, be nothing more than a passage to a life where she doesn't know the alphabet nor where she begins or ends? All she knows is that nothing will ever be like before she carried her first fruit. From now on, nothing will be the same.

♦♦♦

The man, her man, left. She writes to him. Her ideas, her feelings, she lays them down in her beautiful handwriting, in consecutive straight lines. Then she folds the paper and slides it into an envelope. In complete tranquility. Like someone planting seeds into furrows. When she mails them, part of her soul leaves with the letters. Letters which she didn't want to end with periods, but with commas. It pleased her to live as if in the nineteenth century. Romantic, walking toward him with firm steps on a sinuous path between dream and nostalgia.

When they broke up, she stayed home for three days, cut off from everything. Three days to observe the mysterious country deep within herself.

Now, in her own presence, she knows that what happened today is not a consequence of a single break. Because this break was just the gear that shifted certain feelings that had always been buried inside her. The indication of their ascent to the surface. The signal of the fire that's been declared and that's going to ravage everything.

The woman falls to the ground. Her body silently hits the carpet whose lines she followed many times, until she was able to decipher the logic hidden in its entangled signs. Each color. Each movement.

The soul hits death without a noise.

And the soul, does it leave the body then? She rises as she digs a furrow in the air. She extends her whole body, accompanying it to its final destination.

After the whirlwind of words, everything returns to its place. Everything is neutralized in silence: language of the stars running to their ruin.

Blessed is the silence that begins now and will carry on right up to eternity.

This Deliverance

Procreation

Procreation is the only thing that interests nature.

Otherwise, it wouldn't have let the poor exist. Neither the insects with transparent wings nor the prehistoric lizards. Neither anything called rhinoceros, pig, bear, rat, snake, eel. Neither those mysterious animals like tigers (it is often said that whoever can decipher the signs that cover their skin can understand all the enigmas of the universe), praying mantises, animals that can be seen and cannot be seen with the naked eye, peaceful animals, persecuted animals, and even those that tremble at the sight of death. All of them are imprisoned in a whirlwind that reproduces their movement and destiny indefinitely.

Procreation is the only thing that interests nature. Really?

The Big Game

Where does pain come from and where does it go? Pain of individuals that increases with their sensitivity. Pain aroused in you when an animal's throat is slit for you. Pain from someone who is grieving and pain from someone in ecstasy. Pain from childbirth—and always this voice: "You'll give birth in pain." Is this, then, nature's reward for those who secure continuity of the species?

The pain awakens. Because pain does not only come from the exterior but from the depths, from a fire burning inside. Its winds blow from all directions. And pain mixes with fear. Fear of waking up after midnight. Around four o'clock in the morning. At the time when the lights are off and the curtains are lowered. The fear of sleeping adults, not the one of sleeping children... In summary, the temptation to give in to fear when a wonderful lightning strikes the spirit:

"Everything ends up ending," says the Big Game.

The Witness

Shortly after midnight, the public square, changing its atmosphere, begins its secret rites.

Among the numerous knives he possesses, the butcher chooses one, the lightest and most beautiful. The knife is now at the center of the arena, shining in defiance. A unique and luminous stele, a compass directed toward the soul. The butcher raises it to the level of his eyes, contemplates its blade, and immediately tries to caress it with his nail. He brings it near his face and the blade pants.

The slaughtered ox hangs sumptuously on Rembrandt's canvas, as if suspended outside pain and suffering. It is dressed only in the splendor of the brush that painted it. In the public square, the ox to be slaughtered is tied by the legs and thrown to the ground. Moments later, when the rope reaches its neck, after being placed around its legs and ribs, it will comprehend obscurely that it is too late. That it is useless to try to remove the rope from its thick neck and legs. There is nothing to do but succumb to the butcher's knife. And at that moment, just seconds before its throat is cut, the ox lets out a bellow in which death and something beyond death resound in unison. A call, similar to the departure signal of ocean liners before leaving the shore, startling the hearts of travelers who are afraid they'll never come back. Truthfully, it is not just a bellow, but a scream. An extreme, gloomy, eloquent scream.

How can someone witness this scream and not approach it? From what ancestral pain has this scream emerged? Does it allow itself to grind? Does it allow itself to be erased by the air? Or rather, will it hang itself somewhere in the immobile and tranquil air?

And you too, what power do you have when all of a sudden the victims' blood rises in you? Those victims that decorated your childhood with traces of death and held in its sky the bells of the fleeing angel. Bells of mourning.

In the Shadow

We kill in order to eat. We hunt the bird in its sky and the fish in its sea. We slaughter the animal, and uproot the grass.

Someone, in the shadow, is killing us and eating us.

Succumbing to an Ode

The First Abcense

It was the end of September. The sun was more radiant than ever during the beginning of that autumn. After hiking for many hours, my brother reached the summit of the mountain. He climbed for almost an entire day, which he had done twice before, accompanied by his friends who were teenagers like him. The first time he made the journey, he was eleven years old. Since then, he and his friends would make this annual trip to the mountain to end the summer vacation before starting a new school year. On that day, the sun was burning over my brother's uncovered head. The air was extremely fresh and clean. Free like a bird, he leaped over the giant rocks striated with grayish blue and brown tones that enhanced the color of the soil. The bird needs a head covering to protect himself from sunburn as he hops from branch to branch, without a care.

He was very thirsty when he reached the top of the mountain. He leaned over a creek and took a long drink until his thirst was quenched. Then he followed the path to return home and at night began narrating his journey. He was tired, so he promised to continue telling the story the next day and went to sleep. But he never woke up. It was as if he drowned in the water he had refreshed himself with the day before.

I was seven years old at that time. The child that I was didn't realize then what happened to him. It was as if nuclear radiation had penetrated into his body without his knowledge. Continuing along his path, his laughter, his games, without a care. Yet who knows if something was already at work, like some diseases that prepare themselves in secret.

Watching my mother break her usual reserve for the first time in my life was truly disturbing, although I wasn't fully capable of comprehending the gravity of the event. I saw her on the verge of tearing out clumps of her long, loose hair, howling, tearing her clothes in front of everyone, letting everyone see parts of her white skin, hysterically hitting her naked thighs with her palms, screaming like a madwoman. I didn't understand exactly what was happening. I felt like I was under the influence of drugs. Hypnotized, unconcerned. Looking around me without understanding. The continuous screams lasted a whole hour before they transformed into rasping breaths and wails.

Surrounded by some of the closest women to the family, she kept watch all night. There the body laid in bed, and she lay just before him, exhausted from so many tears and keeping vigil, even, for brief moments, forgetting the dead, forgetting herself, allowing her spirit to wander. Her wandering took her to the past, to the beginning of a story of which she remembered only certain chapters. But there she was, suddenly shaking as if she had just woke up from a nightmare. Four hours had already passed. The room was illuminated and the candle too. As for the sky, it was in the same moment of this wonderful clarity, the ultimate moment when the morning star rises at dawn. That dawn was similar in every way to the previous day. Nothing had changed there. Nothing will ever change in the firmament.

On the next morning, family and friends came back to the house, filling the rest of the rooms, except the funerary room which remained always full of women going in and out incessantly. Women who had lost a child at a young age came to participate in the ritual of lamentation and collective mourning. Once in a while, when a man entered the room for a last look, the tone of the weeping and wailing would suddenly increase, giving the impression that these sounds came from a single throat.

Moving around the funeral atmosphere, I began to feel a kind of elation that I could not decipher or know the origin of. It was a drop of happiness amid an ocean of sorrow and visible fates vulnerable, torn. The elder brother lay inside the room, dressed in his best clothes, while I paraded outside among all the friends and relatives who came for a final farewell.

In the kitchen, next to the living room, a group of women were talking. The deceased was the subject to which they constantly returned. They talked while they prepared food for the funeral, with a mix of dedication and concentration. The dishes they prepared were not specific for the occasion. They were dishes commonly prepared on Sundays or holidays, when the family would gather together.

Once in a while, I would approach the door of the room where the women surrounded the death bed. Standing in the middle of the room was the blind singer, the same one who was normally requested for all kinds of ceremonies, joyful or sad. He sang the same songs, be it for weddings or funerals. Nothing changed, neither word nor intonation. They were love songs. Sad love songs that inevitably ended in separation... As for the women, they were not only grieving for the young deceased, but also for the numerous dead that were evoked each time an afflicted mother would arrive. And so the place was transformed into a reunion of parents of the dead gathered for a collective weeping session in which, starting with the death of others, they cried for their own death. Or, by crying for their own dead, they cried for their own death.

We only see the terrifying face of death, yet we know that it has another, one beyond pain and suffering. There, where burning rain falls. There is also the first euphoria there, faded by myrtle and iris water.

My father invites me into the room where, until yesterday, we used to sleep, and which became a stage for the lifeless body. My father enters and starts crying. The relatives and close friends begin to cry in turn. They embrace my father's cry with a forceful liberation of cries. This overflow of cries inside the chests suddenly breaks into a thousand pieces, like broken glass. Adults are the ones who teach children about fear. Why fear? Why do we cry when the body's master is gone? What will happen to him? And who knows what will happen to us? Because of the gentleness around us, we find ourselves in a game that is not ours. We try to cry, for example, in spite of resistant tears. Then, we have no choice but to remain silent and leave this imposing space. Leaving, at the same time, the radiant morning sun, and knowing that from this moment on, we'll never be as we were before. Childhood ends here, all of a sudden. And music's silence dissipates along with its purity before death which, like a fine rain, falls over the world.

My mother is calm now, still outside of herself. Candlelight shines on pale faces accentuating the strangeness. Only my mother, caught up, seems united with some invisible thing. What my mother sees is invisible to the naked eye. Because she sees with her other senses, with her instinct, and how to admit that the branch torn by the storm is completely torn, while the tree is still standing? Does a child really leave his mother's womb? Doesn't he leave some traces that are all anchoring points for a presence that is stronger than any absence? And how could he leave without her if they are like twins, so that he still stirs within her breast, near that place where breath and pulse burst forth?

The voice that was silent for a long time returns, after finally finding its way to the lips and asks the never ending and helpless question: "Why? Who lights this flash of a million colors to extinguish it so soon, stealing its beauty in the blink of an eye? Can that be the rule since the beginning? A rule that we know, yet don't believe in, or rather don't want to believe in, preferring to succumb to fate, only laughing and crying over ourselves."

The mother insists stubbornly, "You say that he left on a trip and that he will come back."

Indeed, he left on a journey. But beyond exile, outside of fear, cold, and waiting. Outside the routine of daily life, beginning with the harshness of work and the misery of money. We dare not say that in the single, most formidable, most authentic moment when someone has just left, going beyond himself and drawing our attention to things that were unknown to us before.

It is truly difficult for a loved one to accept an absence, and yet, on closer inspection, the missing face is not absolute. Sequestered in secret, he turns into a ray of light that bores into us, sheltered from time and temporary lives. He sinks into the heart like streams run deep underground. Softly, sliding through our hearts, he becomes a balm, a soothing agent. He becomes his own consolation.

Now the parents of the deceased were in an advanced state of fatigue. As if they had just overcome the worst of the distance separating them from the cemetery. They had used up their last reserve of tears and cries. It had been thirty hours since the body lay among them. The calm that suddenly reigned over the place was strange, like the calm that follows a fierce battle. A tense and dangerous calm. A noise from the street broke the exhaustion of the assembled, throwing everything into unspeakable disorder. Although we couldn't see it yet, the coffin was there. Wooden, brown. The mother, extending her hand abruptly toward the bed and clinging to it, her eyes wandered over the mortal remains before she hurled herself at them, embracing them, her head against the chest. Is it possible we want to abduct him after so many hours spent in his company? And where would we take him first? The secret desire to keep him right there crossed our minds for a moment.

There were three men trying with difficulty to make their way through the crowd gathered in front of the door of the room, in the direction of the bed, as if they had come to take his life for a second time. At the last moment, right before they proceeded to lift the body, a long cry echoed unexpectedly, followed by a concert of cries, some louder than others. It was like witnessing a collective capital punishment. Where did the cry come from? Exhausted and weak, from where did they get the strength to emit a cry of such bitterness? That cry did not come from the earth, but from below the earth. From its deepest layers. Less than a second passed before suddenly all the women plunged into an overwhelming silence, transformed. They uncovered their heads, untied their hair, and stood, with crazed scowling expressions, as if they were ready to commit an odious crime. Something of the cannibal appeared in their features; hard, terrifying features, reflecting at the same time rage, disgust, repulsion, malediction, dissatisfaction and the feeling of impotence, inequity, and injustice. After everyone rose, they began to distribute the colorful striped shirts of the deceased, waving them as they danced. Meanwhile, the men placed the body inside the coffin. Each part of the body fit inside, finding its place. The head in the place for a head, the arms crossed over the chest, the legs together. Each part carried out its task calmly, methodically, like putting dresses in order in a wardrobe.

The mournful atmosphere, however, did not last long. A kind of communal will wanted us to internalize it, turning it into an intimate matter. A secret shared with others. The days passed by. On some days, when I came home from school earlier than usual I passed the iron gate, threw my school bag over the edge of the sofa, and looked for her in every room. If I got no response, I went out to the balcony overlooking the garden. My eyes wandered until they fixed on a specific place, the corner where the roses grew. After a few moments, I heard my mother's voice at a distance. She was singing. She stayed there, in the shade of the setting sun, singing. That was the place she chose to keep in touch with him. To call him over and over again, as if he were hiding in the corner. To sing for him the same old songs, with a tone at once sad and familiar. The first time I heard those songs, was from the mouths of the mourners before the body. But now her singing was completely different as if it came from another part of her soul. Their meeting was so particular that it took place even after separation.

Abandoning herself in song, in a dual state of absence and contact, she picked a bouquet of roses for him. It was then that I decided to retreat, softly without making any noise each time I came home early. I disappeared into my room, careful not to let her suspect, even for an instant, that I had heard her strange singing. Secret and distant, the scene that took place in the shade provided by the branches of a rosebush should remain as if it happened somewhere far away, in another time and space. I, too, should remain far from this wound that wished to be left uncovered, sheltered from sight. Also, I was cautious never to betray what I had seen or heard. It was unnecessary to have a go at her sense of decency, even less to reveal her amazing discretion.

She had the power to spread joy to everyone. Laughing, playing, joking, clapping, dancing... It was as if she was fooling fate. In hot weather, she sat under the cherry tree at the entrance of the house, where she would warmly welcome the lizard running over the flagstone-paved threshold, inviting it to enter. And when the sun set and the evening breeze made the poplar leaves shake, first she would place her ear next to the tree to hear it whisper, and then she would ask who the recipient of its soft rustling was, for whom the soft song was meant. "Stop, stop," she would say, "The one who loved listening to you already left."

And then, over the course of one of those days, something strange and totally unexpected happened. I arrived home around one o'clock in the afternoon and found no one there. I went to the balcony, hoping to hear her distant incantations. Not a single sound. Only the buzzing of the cicadas that gets louder as the midday sun shines over the orange trees bordering the vast olive field. Having looked everywhere, I heard myself calling her with all my strength. And there she was emerging from a bunch of rosebushes, laughing, swimming like Ophelia in her immaculate whiteness. She was humming, with a bouquet of roses in her hand.

The Second Abcense

Three women enter my bedroom.

I was home alone when they entered. I was sleeping, so I didn't know where everyone had gone. In the space between waking and sleeping, I heard the stifled and interrupted cries resembling the sound of a death rattle. I opened my eyes suddenly to make sure I wasn't dreaming.

I see them covering his small body with a white shawl that belonged to one of the women. A shawl that served as a shroud as well as a final mantle. Three women dressed all in black advancing on tip toe, approaching slowly, then stopping short before my unexpected presence and sudden awakening. The wailing diminished in intensity. Here are three women transformed into three columns and me looking on in fear. I look not only with my eyes, but also with a combined state of sleep and waking, which then is neither sleep nor waking. I looked at them, but they didn't give me the slightest glance. What could they be looking at now? Where do we look at the moment of death?

Realizing that I had woken up for good without a doubt because I looked so bewildered, they began to lament and ululate in one voice, louder and louder. They walked toward me, brandishing the bundle like a threat. I already knew with certainty that what I was experiencing was neither nightmare nor hallucination.

Why take the dead body into the room where I was sleeping? The thirsty baby who didn't sleep through the night before was now a small bundle in the arms of one of the women. I suspected that it wouldn't be long before the bundle would be placed on my bed, that space was in the process of shrinking. Is there enough space in a hole for two bodies? As the space shrinks, the faces become indistinct while the three women stand motionless in the center of the room, as if they have been there forever, long before I fell sleep and long after I woke up, and it was only just now that I noticed. How could I escape from that bundle that hung there under my nose? I leaped in its direction, my quick step contrasting against the women's tense, heavy calm. A movement that breaks their mortal inertia. A strange urge pushed me toward one of the three women, the only one I knew. Her face was sullen and drawn, made up with tears. I approached her, removed the shawl with my shaking right hand, and saw the face at the moment of departure. I looked at it as I would look at a bottomless well. This is how eyesight, when we lose control of our senses, loses balance and starts to wander, inebriated, and the images become blurry, the colors fade, and everything seems to slowly dissolve.

I notice the strange blueness covering his eyes, lips, and the tips of his small fingers. I know that metallic blue color that blends with pale purple. I had seen that color prowling around my older brother who left us, him too, early in life. I replace the cover and draw back. Now, noticing that I am fully awake, I feel my fear grow. I dressed quickly. The three women stood between me and the door that I had to pass through to reach the landing and fresh air, which I quickly realized was still trapped inside the lungs of the dead baby.

I didn't return home for two days, thinking that enough time had passed for the house to return to its initial cleanliness, before being filled with the smell of death. And for the sun to return, so it could filter through the rooms, as was usual in summer, through the shutters, before disappearing behind the tall trees.

Much later, I found out that the three women placed the baby on my bed to change him, dressing him in the all white outfit he wore on his first birthday, washing his forehead with orange flower water, combing his curly hair. In any case, what I never knew, and will probably never know, is what my mother was doing on that morning. Could she have fled the house, like I did, only to return two full days later long enough to bury the child's body and his shadow?

On returning home, I felt a crazy urge to get my hands on a trace of the baby who left: a piece of clothing, a toy, the little red car he never let go of, caressing it constantly, sometimes putting it in his mouth and filling it full of drool, frightening my mother who feared he might swallow it. She would take it from him and then give it back to him immediately when he insisted...

When he was taken to the cemetery, they took all traces of him along as well. Even his pictures were taken out of the frames. From that day on, nothing was left to indicate his presence or preserve his memory. However, what I really found strange was the way my mother welcomed me on the night I returned home. She seemed radiant, as she usually was. She didn't mention what happened. Neither the death of the the little one nor my absence from home. As if nothing had happened. As if the infant who came to replace the other, the first to disappear, and whose name he was made to bear, one would say that he had hardly come at all.

That was the second absence. The first one, completely unforeseen, struck without notice. Anyway, even with notice, death is always unpredictable. And it always strikes too soon. It was the month of September. The last hot days in the high mountains.

Every death is a homicide. Even a natural death.

Your fire didn't last long, little one. Only the length of one passion to another. From that of the spring to that of the estuary. Barely outlined by light, the ashes erase you. Yet, a tender voice cradles you. Tireless, eternally young, a voice that dust cannot cover.

Cape of Hope

When the first ship released its mooring lines there was no land in sight. The sea was its own point of departure, that and some branches floating on its surface. The people on board had no precise destination. It was enough for them to sway on the water. This was long before memory and expectation, millions of years ago.

The sea became agitated with expectation and the waves roared. The color of the sky changed and a borderline rose between the beginning and the end. Between man and woman. Between the desire for paradise and the fear of hell.With expectation, fear moved in, rendering the cape of hope indispensable, it doesn't matter, it makes no difference.

The storm and the rain subsided. The night came and with it lanterns. And the stars finished their circuit, definitively fixing the position of the earth. And this began to spin. From then on, the traveler became aware that he was only a shadow of a tree, and that long before he existed, the journey had already begun.

The sun rises and sets. The snow falls in winter and summer makes the mountains switch between orange and purplish-blue just before the day washes up in the secret of the mute valleys that draw the dividing line between the sea and the high mountains.

At midday the power of the sun is such that the landscape disappears behind a hazy white veil. The colors blend and dissipate. The mountain there becomes more than an ethereal image, illuminated.

This is genesis, but before color.

It is necessary to wait for night so this place can find its fullness and majesty, with the appearance of the star that announces the opening ceremony. It is at that moment that this place is closest to the fingers of the Creator. Shortly after, at night fall, which masks the top and sides of the mountains, millions of stars make their entrance into the scene in perfect order, from east to west and from north to south. They advance slowly, moving from one side to another, with caution. Like a ballet.

The twinkling wounds of the darkness are about to ooze, inundating the other side of space. But we only see the quivering. Like a clown, a meteor crosses the open space, this gigantic arena—wonderful and inspiring. Meanwhile, the meteor knows no beginning or end. As if it was there only to affix its signature to the summit of the celestial vault. And to burst out laughing.

To let the world know that war, war on earth, is its nourishing mother.

The Corpse's Dream

It was night, when the house was submerged in sleep, that I heard the sound of the river. It arrived by way of the orange and olive trees, bearing their perfume to me. And so, traversing my dreams, the river watched over me. I woke up suddenly, after a nightmare, to the sound of splashing, and I felt it running near me, whispering, "Don't be afraid."

I spent my childhood in the company of that river. In spite of its constant murmuring, it knew how to listen to me. In the winter, it came from far away, at the same time as the black clouds. During clear dawns, I looked in the direction of the mountains for the slightest sign announcing their arrival. I decorated my first library with the reeds bordering the river. That river was my guide and teacher. My friend and messenger whom I loaded with missives destined for the sea and its predictable travels.

The approaching autumn, its trees, leaves, and celestial colors is like approaching a tiger behind bars. Although formidable, the tiger is beautiful. Beautiful, Schubert's "Fantasy" for piano. Not only can someone listen to his distress, but also that of the whole world. From near or far, one also hears a whine, reaching the ear from behind the seas and oceans. The whine of those drowned in future centuries. Of those who will be born already drowned.

It happens sometimes, when we are in one specific time and place, that we feel like we are in all times and places. Not in the sense that we are or could be eternal, but in the sense that we would be able to deploy the totality of our energy, in a sense to be, in a flash of lightening, in tune with the infinite.

This is how the river comes to me, from an open window over the prairies, the wild rosebushes, the brambles, the thistles, the anemones. As I watch it run, I unfailingly return to the top of the mountain and climb to its first gestures. And this mountain, at an angle facing the neighboring mountain of cypresses, seems to give free rein to the quiet summer village that lives at its feet—without the mountain, the village would have moved to the bottom of the valley. During the daytime, this mountain is a focal point for itself and everything that surrounds it. At night, the cypresses sink there and the olive greens interlace with the dark browns, before transforming, with the first light of day into a wheat yellow cameo. One would think that colors are the only thing that concerns the mountain. From morning to night. From the first light of the day until the violet hour. Between that interval of time, an infinite blueness fills the sky with gradations, marking its borders with a grayish touch that imprints the valley on rocks and hermitages. Day and night, in a constant movement, the colors of this mountain are made and unmade. Trying to attain perfection—it is actually sculpted with absolute perfection—it seems to be constantly looking for an ideal form. It never loses contact with what happens in the depths of the earth or outside, where the wind and its burins are in action, secretly corroding it. Then, light as a veil, a white cloud passes by, swirls around it, caresses its high peak, and then disappears. In September, the mist invades it. It is during this month when it withdraws to the valley to spend the night and to cry secretly, leaving behind a mountain that seems like a hoisted sailboat, a floating iceberg, a lighthouse for travelers without destination.

I was born at the foot of this mountain. Very near its rocks and dandelions. It was there where I opened my eyes to the first wars. To the wars of rival families and insatiable vengeance. Also to the hatred of two neighboring villages on the mountain and at the seashore. That hatred which years later appeared before my face as a civil war. I have seen piles of corpses being kicked by exhausted combatants. They kicked the heads of the corpses, whose extremities couldn't fit in the trucks that drove through the streets followed by a crowd, as in a procession. As the trucks passed, women made the sign of the cross, standing in their houses, surrounded by their children. A woman held an image of the Virgin Mary, which she removed from a wall of her living room. Waving the image from left to right, she stopped for a moment to begin her prayers, screaming and howling. Meanwhile, the elderly came out of their houses, astonished, silent, hypnotized, holding candles that revealed the features of their worried faces.

A priest headed the procession. Dressed in a black cassock covered by a cloth embroidered with golden thread, he marched slowly, swinging a large censer. The smoke released by the incense made the atmosphere even more mysterious, more unreal. Now, the prayers and supplications were mixed with the screams of victory that the crowd uttered in unison. The priest, with a purple face, advanced in the distance. He seemed like he was floating above the smoke as the crowd kept coming from everywhere. For a moment, as he moved, he and his revolver disappeared from sight and then, an instant later, part of his cassock and lengthy stole, which fell over his shoulders like a waterfall, could be seen again. His face, always changing according to his mood, remained calm further on, as if fixed on a precise object. I saw his eyes fixed on an invisible point, a place where in order to enter one must have exercised prayers and meditations for a long time. Amid the whitish cloud of incense, the priest was just two subjugated eyes.

The entourage stopped at the public square where the priest began preaching. He stood above the corpses while the combatants, obstructed by their weapons, surrounded him. One of them asked him, "And what should we do now?" The priest replied, "The will of God." Then he continued, "We will exterminate every last one... We will make them taste hemlock until their bile sweetens, and we will destroy their houses over their heads." As he said that, spitting and frothing at the mouth, the priest looked in all directions. And as he raised his voice, the ardor of the people increased. Some, losing control, threw themselves on the corpses to kick and spit on them.

The noise could be heard from afar. The roaring of a war that was happening somewhere else. In a place where, undoubtedly, another truck carried corpses of another religious belief. The air shrank. The sky also shrank. I turn to you then, oh, my mountain. You who observe us in silence from afar, you see how the fear of death is so great in us that we kill each other, that we make of this a game. In vain, I take flight, a giddy fleeting cloud, to see you. Dazzled by the power of the shining sun, I turn to you. You are there, while I am from nowhere. I implore you because you see, at your height, what I can't see. I can't even see the sea or the waves that draw the movement of my days. Oh, mountain, it is to you and only to you whom I have trusted my childhood in the vigil of my departure. Who is a better guardian than you?

I was already far away when I received the photograph of the combatants kicking the corpses. I saw it with terror and eagerness. I looked at the faces of the killers and the victims. I knew, one by one, all of those who had claimed the power to end human lives. As I looked at them closely, a touch of the divine could in fact be read on their faces.

This photograph posed before me summarizes the war. The killer and the victim together in the same frame. One next to the other. The victim lies on the truck, with his head facing down. The killer holds this head with his boot. Standing in a defiant position, he holds his rifle as he looks at the camera. By doing that, he defies not only an enemy or any human being, but death itself. The strength and determination of the hands that hold the weapon firmly, and the tension that enhances the prominence of the veins in the face and neck are in contrast with the serene face of the victim. While the killer gives the impression that he wants to possess the victim in body and soul, the victim, on the contrary, behind his half-closed eyes, shows a face finally calmed, as if he has found a strange tranquility, as if he were trapped in a light that doesn't belong to this world. This relaxed face under a boot seems to be sleeping and dreaming in a wheat field. His face is not pale, unlike the faces of corpses. There isn't a trace of suffering that preceded the execution, of anguish for the imminent death, but instead, there is sweetness, tenderness, compassion... At the edge of the photograph, there is another face that seems joyful with victory, someone with a sign of arrogance in the corner of his lips. A false arrogance that nevertheless seems prudent, dubious, and perhaps unwilling to reveal itself. One more face, this one here, shows an uneasy smile and a pair of eyes evading the cliché. Among the numerous faces, there is also one of a terrified woman looking at all the corpses being kicked.

Now, far from that space and time, I ask myself: Why would someone want to capture the rays of a setting sun and restlessly chase them, one by one, with his eyes? Is it because he wishes to depart along with the last one of these rays?

Carnival

They took us to the front to die, but not all of us are dead. Those who did die became martyrs. We have withdrawn then, from ourselves, ashamed of being still alive.

They told us, "Don't be ashamed, a lost battle is not a lost war. You'll be the nourishment for future battles." Therefore, we were grateful to the Almighty.

A moment later, the captain screamed, "Each one of you, take this deadly weapon in your hand." Then he opened The Book and started reading, "A man dressed in linen and with an inkwell hanging at his side will march among you. First, he'll reach the center of the city, then you'll follow him and attack. None of you shall know mercy, not even your eyes, so don't spare anyone. Not even the elderly, young girls, children, or women. Attack until everyone is dead. Start with the elderly in front of their houses. Fill the houses with corpses. Go."

We marched. With a smile on our lips, anger in our souls, and a strong desire in our hearts to use our daggers. To stab or be stabbed. To kill or be killed. Each of us took on a quasi-human shape, hiding somehow the despicable animal that had revived in us.

We heard, "We are the flesh. Advance." We advanced.

Among us, "The man dressed in linen and with an inkwell hanging at his side" marched as well.

We advanced, making the ground echo under our steps, filling the space with our chants, rolling the drums with fervor. Then, one of us started to cry because the terrible procession was delayed and he had lost his patience.

They told us, "Kill and dismember." And our enemies, before us were told to kill and dismember too. "Exterminate," we were told. "Exterminate," our enemies were told. In that evening march to the slaughter, we partied. What was just sand and mirage was now, an army marching toward us. Suddenly, we found ourselves again about to wage a battle with knives, stabbing and being stabbed, exchanging mysterious kisses among us. Martyrdom has never been so close. Our blood ran and we laughed about it. Our eyes popped out of their orbits and we laughed about it. We knew, in open combat, that satellites spied on us and transmitted all this uproar live. Aware that the people sitting in front of their TV sets expected a lot from us, we were careful not to disappoint them. Therefore, did not pull any punches, mowing down heads, tearing arms, and looking at wounds, with impudent eyes, almost in ecstasy. When the carnival came to an end and the noise of the weapons incited us to dance, we danced until we couldn't anymore and our exhausted bodies, after the combat, fell on top of the corpses. As we found no one else to kill, we started looking for pieces of raw flesh among the dead bodies. To take the disaster into our own mouths, to drink to disaster, and to build kingdoms of dust.

To the expression "To be or not to be, that is the question," we replied, "To be or not to be, that is the derision."

We advanced. A great fear protected us from fear. The spectacle of the enemies' decomposing bodies immunized us against decomposition. Massacring, just asking ourselves if amid the laying masses there was enough space for all this death in us. Finally, we wore the shirts of the dead: our most beautiful path to death.

The battle ends, but the combat continues.

As long as a woman gives birth, the combat will continue.

As long as a woman gives birth, the hordes will draw a line of blood on the horizon.

The Lamentation of the Beast

The night fell on us heavily. It was of a strange darkness which stuck to our fingers and to the whites of our eyes. We were home, silent, each one of us crouched in anguish and fear. Fear before the fear that came from prehistoric times. Fear of the beast that is about to be killed. I didn't sleep that night. The feeling of imminent killing prevented my eyelids from closing. How can one sleep when war and killers are everywhere? It was as if they were ordered to shoot at anything on land capable of moving. Starting with the living beings escaping in fear: men, dogs, cats, and even the tree branch moving in the emptiness. It was as if they were ordered to exterminate instantly everything that trembled. From then on, every movement was persecuted. The city had been agitated for too long—it had been a long time since it came to a halt. Hundreds, thousands of bullets on the walls, trees, and clouds. Although one bullet per person would have sufficed, some bodies were riddled with dozens of them as if to increase death, while other bodies were cut and burned, and then the ashes spread in distant regions. Hence, ash and dust became indistinguishable.

I didn't sleep that night. Shortly after midnight, I heard a scream at a distance and slowly, it came closer to our house. It wasn't the noise of the water coming from the river, but a scream coming from the other side of the hill in front of our house. Or rather, was that scream coming from inside us? It lasted a long time and its echo continued to resound in a thousand places, as if coming from the four corners of the planet. The night was empty and we lay in wait, as is usual when fear grows. At that moment, we were almost able to perceive the sap ascending a tree, a plant emerging through the cracks of the dry soil, the blood running through our veins. The depths of the earth shaking in our own depths.

The scream that shattered the night was both continuous and discontinuous. It turned from groaning to howling. When someone suffers to that extent, it is impossible to scream like a man, but like a dog. There was a mixture of human and animal lamentation in that scream emitted by someone who was suffering. And then a sudden silence. Following the scream, the silence was painful, loaded, as if embalmed with fear and death. To me, that silence was as terrible as the scream before it. Even more, it was marked by mystery, strangeness, unbearable burden. The silence turned inward, to his heart whose pulsations become a discontinuous scream. A tense scream as powerful as an iron hammering in a closed space. A scream stifled inside that must escape at any cost. However, regardless of whether it might stay inside or be able to escape, death is already announced. This is the nightmare that you see with open eyes...

Then, suddenly, thundering screams crossed the wall of the world. That night of my life summarizes the night of the world, always and forever.

On the following day, waking up from a sleepless night, from a wound that I wished had made me silent forever, no one made reference to what was heard from midnight to dawn. As if what happened were unspeakable. As if it were a matter of rape or incest. As if it were excrement that must be hidden or thrown away secretly, out of sight. Not until two days later, a local newspaper reported the incident in a few lines:

"Seven people of this religious belief were tortured and murdered on the hill next to the river to avenge the death of other people of that other religious belief."

To have come so close to death without dying and yet to testify. When death is so close, it oozes out through our pores and yearns to gaze the first light of dawn. I didn't close my eyes that night. Nor the following nights. And if I did sleep, I would wonder, when I woke up, if I had really slept, since part of my dreams and sleep were filled with screams by the tortured at the moment of their last breath. They move away slowly from their own scream. I see them, as I would see them on a canvas by Goya, raising their impotent arms to protect themselves from the executioner's bullets. I see them dying their first and last death. Who could ever keep count?

Only after the war is over can we say that we are alive. Or maybe when we can evaluate what is dead or still alive in us. A difficult task, since it is hard to classify the survivors of a war. Are those who have seen with their own eyes dead or alive? An eye that has seen death, can it still see? That eye that trembles at the weak ray of light entering through a window. That eye stained by the whiteness of absence, by an empty expression... Then the other eyes. Those that observe us from behind bars and no longer belong to this world. Survivors of death. Therefore, are we survivors of those expressions that will forever torment us? How and where do we find shelter? Can the wounded be protected from his own blood?

We let the future unveil itself with hands open in the mist. We move forward in a tunnel of growing darkness. There was no electricity in those mountain villages where we found refuge away from the war that broke out in the city and then in the whole country. That is why we didn't know about it. There had been no electricity since the beginning of the war and most certainly not before it either. The glow of the stars twinkles above an immense whiteness. Between mountains, we are as if between two parts of a book of snow. From now on, the candles of prayer and supplication are now candles of light. Vivid and trembling light that will keep us company throughout the storm, like a friend. Amused by our joy frightened by our fear, suddenly accentuating it. Like us, it was sensitive to the cold, the humidity, and the breeze that betrayed the crack in the wall.

We let the future unveil itself...

In This Voice Your Star and Ash

It is the first dusk after the trip. In the iris of the night, the sky is blue. A tree emptying itself of its sap can be seen with the naked eye. You hear it say, "Come closer, my friend." For a second time, it is a woman's voice that shows you the way. Her voice between your star and your ash. It is your first home, the roof over your head and soul. What is there to do in that place? We are made of matter that substitutes distant homes and lost places with familiar faces since childhood. And these faces sharpen the tips of the wind and the dew. They are what you drink and eat. What lives and dies in you every instant. From now on, this voice will come every night, once everyone is sleeping: "In your absence, I will take you to a place higher than the one children are taken to. And like those children, I will wait for you."

I left twenty years ago. It was afternoon nap time. We had just finished lunch, although no one had really touched their plates. Everyone was just pretending to eat. The car was parked in front of the garden door; the driver hadn't moved from his place. My brother carried the luggage while I said goodbye to family members, close friends, and some neighbors gathered in the yard and the balcony overlooking the garden. I hugged each person, adults as well as children. Finally, I made my way toward my mother, who was sitting next to the door. She embraced me with all her strength and covered me with kisses. Only after I walked through the door did I realize that she was almost motionless while she embraced me. She didn't move from her chair, she didn't join the rest of the people. With eyes fixed on the front door of my house, I got inside the car and sat next to the driver. Everyone stood at the door, waving their hands. I did the same. After the car started and made a U-turn, I was still looking at the front door of my house. My mother was there, standing, supporting herself with her left hand on the door frame. Suddenly, she raised her other hand and started to call my name, with all her strength.

It wasn't a call but more like a scream. A resounding cry similar to that of roots being ripped out. A scream identical to the one she emitted on the day she said goodbye to her eldest son being dragged inside his coffin to his final destination. That scream was the last thing I carried with me from a land destroyed by the fire of a devastating war. Like a surprising call, years later, that scream still resounded inside me, even though the war had already ended a long time ago. That scream still startles me today, as if it is still hitting my eardrums. I wouldn't be surprised if my mother herself has forgotten that scream, so sorrowful, evolving inside me like a living thing. Yet, I have never dared to remind her of that goodbye. Even better than me, she should be able to decipher that sign.

Before your eyes, a tree empties itself of its sap. Its leaves tremble in the wind. Spreading themselves in all directions. While you just keep looking in the same direction. The one the soft breeze comes from. I left twenty years ago and since that first day a candle has been lit. A candle that she relights every day. From the moment she opens her eyes, she's already preparing for the mystery of the following day. For my mother this flame represents my presence at home. What will be left of me there, the day that flame goes out?

Women are endowed with the power of limitless love. That kind of love that expects nothing in return, that knows neither the misery of impatience nor the disappointment of an unfulfilled rendezvous. That doesn't know the metamorphosis of age and consequences for the body and the spirit, which never changed in her heart. Such is a mother's love. A quiet love like evening shadows on still water, blue and golden. A kind of sleeping letter in the limbo of an intimate sea.

Now, my mother is there by herself, sitting quietly in a corner, accompanied by her angels. The incense fills the house with thick smoke that disappears in the distance. I was able to see her angels several times. It was in those moments that peace filled her heart and serenity filled her eyes, a serenity not of this world. Now she is there, sitting in the same corner as twenty years ago. I see her from far away. I see the angels flying around her like birds around bread crumbs on the open palm of a child proud of his new outfit on a festive day. The strangest thing is that after years of war, her habits haven't changed at all. For example, during my several visits, she behaved exactly like she did before the war and before my long trip. At night, she perfumed my bed with jasmine flowers and orange blossoms. In the morning, she watched over my sleep and scared away the birds with her scarf, forcing them to sing somewhere farther away. Nevertheless, the birds kept warbling, perched high in the trees, as if unnoticed, making fun of that woman who is still, nowadays, a hostage of a strange amazement...

"How can I sleep when the contradictions in my heart are awake?" she says, pushing open the door of the large balcony. There, she looks at the sky and finds the farthest place. Then she turns her head from left to right, as if washing her face in the light of the stars. Those stars she loves above everything that make her slowly delirious.

She stands at the balcony and talks to them between midnight and dawn. She implores them, believing they listen to her intently. And while she gazes at the Milky Way, a meteor passes by. Messenger of flame to extinct stars, it furrows the sky and conjugates it in the past tense.

Ebb and Flow of a Gemstone

The Angel of the Last Instant

Here is the music you love so much. It often begins before our meetings. The music passes through the thin walls as if slipping through fingers or pores in the skin. The music by Mozart. Concerto No. 23. The piano plays prudently and softly; each touch freed slowly from its binding. It doesn't cry or wail, but penetrates into the flesh, probing its depths. It is neither the touch of a meeting nor the touch of a farewell. It is the music of the gaze that deviates from foreseeable endings.

Often times, the music would start but would not end. I didn't let it end. It trembled in my hands, bringing it to its point of departure, as if insisting on returning a river to its source. The morning of waiting had passed entirely and then, suddenly, everything became a blur. Unnoticed, the rhythms came one after another, freely, peacefully, until the end. I opened the window and I looked at the sky. A blue sky on the twentieth of July, the day of your sixty-third birthday. I waited for the lonely white cloud to leave.

How can the musician play when the person whose birthday you're celebrating isn't there? It's not like her to be late. Did she misunderstand the rendezvous point? She would be in the process of setting the table, preparing the glases for the travelers, which they raise without suspecting that it might be for the last time.

You happily announced your next trip. This time, to Asia. The trip will be long; it will take hours and hours. I didn't protest. How can I complain when you tell me about it so happily? I didn't even ask you how you would find the strength for such a trip. But your voice, which sparkles with a thousand lights, here it was extinct after a sip of wine, and your gaze lost in emptiness. This sip of wine took you to a place where I couldn't meet you. Returning from a moment of distraction, it is as if you came back without your life, having left it where you had drifted off. I never knew where that deep redness would take you. You would drink wine, mouthful after mouthful, while the veil of deep sadness invaded your eyes. Is it sorrow for the time that had passed or rather pain of an unknown origin that ties you and takes control of you?

The last time we met, you were just returning from a trip to Greece. You were tired. You told me that you would not leave Paris for a long time. You walked quietly by my side with a sickly slowness that revealed how tired your body was as you walked. Something quite different from the way you usually moved. Your incandescent voice became weaker and weaker after each meeting. Meetings I desired the more I sensed that something was abandoning you. "I'm going to Indonesia and I'll tell you what I see." Instead of asking you the reason for this surprising trip to such a remote place, I was happy to capture the echo of the country's name. The warmth of your voice gave me the illusion of your capacity to make the trip.

We agreed to see each other again on your birthday, to go to the movies to see "The Red Violin", then to walk around the edge of the lake in the Bois de Boulogne, where you liked to talk about René, who left you two years ago. You told me once that you never understood him until he left. We felt a need to hug him in spite of the space and silence. To see him even though he is in heaven, floating in inaccessible places. You used to say that he was the architect of everything he did. And that he could see everything with the eyes of an architect. He who came from Greece, with an inscription of Plato on his forehead: "God himself is an architect." You loved to simplify and change the quote. "God is architecture," you would say.

The last time, we stayed in the living room until evening. Amid the sea green color of that night, we had the impression of being in a giant aquarium. Slowly, the room became dark, but we chose not to turn on the light. We were together, yet absent from each other. What united us was something we were hiding from each other; we knew that since the beginning. Like our dreams, that thing did not have a fixed habitat. It stayed outside us, in those rigid homes that devour our flesh and suck our blood without ever becoming satiated. Nouba, your white dog, had the habit of walking around in the semidarkness of the growing night, jumping on the pillows, resting on the chair next to the TV set, coming near me to catch my cap with his snout, letting it fall, catching it again, and then running, overly excited to make a toy out of my cap. On that day, we didn't laugh as we normally did when Nouba was with us. We were distracted in the house that embraced the shadow of the night with open arms. The house that witnessed our union and disunion. Turning toward you, I couldn't see your face clearly. In the darkness, time started acting secretly. I was afraid and I invited you to have dinner at the restaurant next door, The Vodevil.

During this meeting where you were elegant and wore more makeup than usual everything that was hidden in us was revealed. You told me how you took the train to Marseilles, then how you recovered René's ashes before boarding a boat with your daughter that had taken you to the sea where you had spread the contents of the urn. And without asking, you told me that it was you who chose that place, because it is in the Mediterranean Sea. The waves will undoubtedly deliver René, a son of light, back to his homeland.

It was Nouba, your companion in your last days, who found you laying on your back a moment after our telephone conversation on that Thursday morning. It was eleven o'clock in the morning. A ray of light, crossing the room, from one side to another, passes over your knees. Nouba approaches you, turns to you, waits for a sign, a sound, a caress. Soon it will be time for the daily walk. And you, where are you then?

And Nouba? What happened to Nouba?

You are no longer part of the visible world. In short, you are no longer in the world. You neither left for a trip nor came back to tell me about it. What you hoped, the sudden spurt from the heart of night, like a face that comes into the world between your hands, like a living flame in your body, you took it with you when you left. You didn't have enough time to gather, at the bottom of the glass, the remains of your despair, disappointment, love, joy and beauty. Or even those tears shed for God when the angel of the last instant forgot to appear. You are alone, there, in that vast space carrying your body with the strength left in you, carrying it with increasingly heavy steps toward a quiet bed, without sadness or pain. You put it to bed as you would put a child to bed when he wants to sleep. You are watchful that every limb is in place. You raise your right hand slightly, you observe it out of the corner of your eye before closing your eyes again, whispering, "I depart." You depart, like one closes the shutters when night falls. Or like one closes a book when one has just finished reading.

From your house to Notre-Dame-des-Victoires, some meters we had traveled many times, along the neighboring public garden. We walked through the narrow alley to the big square next to Gallery Vivienne, where we drank tea with cinnamon. Despite the age difference between us, our memories shared a common trunk. Sitting there, remembering, we realized that what we had lost never really belonged to us, which relieved us of any need of consolation, of any hope of resurrection.

From your house to the church, I look for you in pure abstraction. In the unfigurable. In the brightness of a star over high clouds. Even higher. In the dawn reflected on the mountains, waking up a sleeping spirit. The music you loved so much is about to start. It usually starts before we meet. The musical tune starts when the musicians are absent.

The table was set; the candles and funeral flowers everywhere. Everyone was there but me. Since I couldn't ask, I will never know in which sea your ashes have been spread. Nor in which seas our common illusions remain.

Around the Pyramid

It was our last trip to Cairo. We knew it, and we also knew that we would never see each other again. However, we acted as though this meeting, which took place after a long separation, was going to be decisive. The city, with all its angels and demons, offered us a sight that no other city could offer. The mosques and fountains, the mausoleums and faces. Where do all these sacred stones come from? Who brought them here, transforming them into passageways to another life, to a hope that poses no harm and comes to us effortlessly in every gene and bud?

The city and its stones. Also, the day has its stones. The night and the air too. What are we here to do and what are we searching for amid the colonnades and monuments? You repeat the name of the places with delight: Al-Aqmar, Al-Ghawri, Ibn Tulun, Sultan Hassan... We walk from one monument to another, from one face to another. You laugh. I hear your laughter echoing in my heart and on the marble. And the city that emerged and stood for thousands of years is suddenly vulnerable, soft, and ready to fall at any moment, amid the undulations of your laughter. It was our vulnerability that we perceived in all these things.

Love comes to us, but we possess nothing of it. Because love comes from nowhere, while we do come from somewhere. And how can we possess what cannot be possessed? Every time we are about to touch the light of someone we love, the veil gets torn and we wake up. Everything takes flight and dissipates, like those distant clouds. And what escapes from us is another mirage of our lost paradises. The earth was vast not too long ago, and the world opened its arms to me. I ran toward it like a child. Are they my father and my mother? Not too long ago, I had two parents and the idea that life was just an instant. Not Rome with its squares, not Pompeii baptized by the fire of Vesuvius, nor that mosaic in which a naked woman, straddled on a man, holds his penis as if it were the trunk of a tree that she puts back into the soil. Nothing in the world resembles Cairo, which travels through the epochs in the blink of an eye, from the pyramids of Giza to the Coptic convents, passing through the Fatimid, Ayyubid, and Mamluk monuments. It was in Cairo where I found you and lost you. I was not successful in gathering between my two palms all the ages hung in the great hall of this familiar place.

We saved the last day for the pyramids. Once we arrived, we had the vague impression that we had not come here from somewhere else, or even that we had never left this place in our lives. We were silent during the journey, our eyes riveted by these in the tight harmoniously aligned stones. Every stone is a panel, and every panel is a message where the fire of our primeval memory is incubated. We swayed on the sand as we would on a camel's back, without looking at each other. Together, we looked at one single point, that invisible point of the pyramid where the secret of past generations is kept for generations to come. Each of us, by gazing toward the height of the pyramid, was looking at ourselves.

The rays of the midday sun resembled a rain of fire descending the steps of the pyramid toward my face. I felt dizzy, and my perception of things and living beings around me became blurred: the sand, the camel, the woman. I imagined the pyramids on a celestial body abandoned by its inhabitants who took their luggage and belongings, but didn't worry about leaving the stones. Nevertheless, the pyramid was there, on our earth, and we were there, leading the entourage. We approached the pyramid and touched the stones, as if trying to read what absence had written there. As if trying to test the depth of its external layer, with a bit of intuition and memory as the only instruments of measurement. Touching them was like touching four thousand years combined in a fraction of a second, knowing that what we were contemplating there in that moment had never been and would never be the same with the passage of years.

The message reached us. Its mummified death reached us. What is there to do? The pyramids reached us and there we were before them, looking at their highest point and not seeing anything. The point that faces the sky comes from the sky and not the earth. It comes from the boundaries where the reading of languages failed. But this is not about hieroglyphs, or Arabic, or Latin. The journey is still in its beginning and these languages communicate just the babbling of the beginnings.

Before arriving at this pyramidal structure built on four triangular bases and a single peak, the architect thought about several hypotheses and conceived different shapes. Like every artist before executing a work of art. Like the one who created Gilgamesh's ship. Like Piero della Francesca or Giorgio di Chirico. Like Dürer before finding instruments of measurement for his engraving "Melencolia I". When he found them, he saw a winged being with a compass in hand and a guardian angel at its side. That being began to contemplate man's fate and his limited knowledge. There is a magic square with numbers above its head, a sphere at its feet, and around it, a balance, a bell, a sun dial, and a sand clock. The artist gathered so many instruments in the engraving to portray melancholy and make an allusion to time.

Searching for the purest and most perfect shape, the ideal shape, the ancient Egyptian architect thought of something that had no beginning or end. He thought of the circle from which he would have extracted a spherical representation. Enclosed in its secrets which possess both the rational and irrational, the circle is the image of the sun, the full moon, and the woman's womb, symbol of fertility and giving. He spent entire nights studying the relationship between the circular shape and the place, between the place and the reflection of the sun on the smooth surface at dawn and dusk. But the sphere reveals a celestial body and a celestial body needs a satellite to move; otherwise, the magnificent sphere would collapse. This sphere, to be considered one of the Seven Wonders of the World, would fall on the surface of the earth like a great, intangible, calcified tear drop. At the image of this strange tear, the architect stepped back, wondering if the earth wasn't that tear itself. And then, tears are characteristic of Adam's children, the result of ancient sensations and feelings. That's when he had the idea of the square. The square is elegant, of equal sides. However, the joy of this discovery didn't last long because he found it pretentious, self-sufficient, and didn't offer a notable difference between its construction and destruction.

The spirit of the architect dissipated in an instant. A golden blue color striated the sky, producing a great shadow over the earth; then, slowly, losing its golden tone, it turned into deep dark blue, masking the brightness. The first star occupied its place in the sky. At the remaining light of the day, the architect lay on the ground, opened his hand on the sand, and with great fear, as if he had found a treasure, took a handful of it and began to work. He began by drawing a straight line, followed by another three, and then he joined them. Four straight, symmetrical lines. Next to this square, on a horizontal position, he drew the sacred double square. The architect then went back to what he had put aside, the square, which was the essential base for his architecture and monument. But how could he apply measurements, dimensions, logarithms, and other divine proportions to something terrestrial? The square as the base then. The Aleph. But what could be placed on top and how could the Aleph be completed? He looked at the sky again, convinced that architecture was born from gazing at the sky.

He knew where he would build his monument, but not what shape it would take. He left his family, his friends, his town, and went to the chosen place to examine it. The sand dunes offered him a blank page. Something called him from the deepest part of that stripped area. He set up a tent where he spent three consecutive days and nights. On the third night, exhausted by the effort and insomnia, he looked at the sky and noticed that the stars were in an unusual state of disorder. He immediately closed his eyes and placed his palms on them. He remained in this position for a long time. Suddenly, half asleep, he saw something that looked like a full vulva, jet-black, with a twinkling labia. The ray of light that acquired the shape of an inverted triangle made the heart of the triangle even more mysterious and magical. In what way would this place for birth be transformed into a place for death? And why not make this passage that brings us to earth, a point of departure to heaven? The architect was contemplating all this when a sandstorm destroyed the tent, throwing away its contents and scattering over the boundaries of the desert the instruments of measurement and the blank papyrus devoid of any line, of any letter.

Nevertheless, the thing he was approaching was not a line but a volume. And the volume is the pyramid. Like the sphere comes from the circle, the pyramid derives from the triangle. And from the pyramid derives the obelisk. He understood then that the pyramid could not exist without three lines of extreme simplicity and perfection. From the middle of the earth, at its central point, the pyramid rises, certainly in a dialogue with the polar star. At equinox, the sunlight hits an angle in the south, uncovering a hollow, nothing hazardous, barely visible. Could that be a clue to what is hiding inside, and is it an invitation to force the entrance? But how could someone enter when all the doors are closed? How could someone open a gap in the air and escape through it?

A light rain fell on the day that work on the pyramid was completed. As if to wash the stone from the wounded prints and the suffering of the hands that built it. It rained the whole day before the sunlight appeared again with all its strength and the desert began to put its sand in order. Every grain of sand in its place. Except that since the pyramids were built, the desert has never been the same. Since then, from the top of the pyramid, man has uttered a scream. He does it after he strips himself of his flesh, bones, and blood and becomes as light as a handful of air. Also, from this part of the pyramid, life and death lose their meaning, and henceforth love and hatred, joy and sadness, war and peace. It is there where the pyramid starts. From this attraction between the earth and everything above it. From four triangles whose long extremities find their bases on four lines. The pyramid is man's first temple after his emergence from the darkness of the caves. It is the first encounter with the sky. It is the mausoleum of the world.

The building of the pyramids did not stop there. From the Tower of Babel to the Ziggurats and to Cape Canaveral, there is one single preoccupation. From the most ancient and harmonious architectural lines of Mesopotamia to the countries of the Fertile Crescent and to Egypt and Greece. From the sacred view of the creation of the world to the creation of modern technology, which is absent of all metaphysics, man has always looked heavenward. To what can potentially contribute to his salvation. To the source of light where there is no need to look with open eyes in order to see. "Close your eyes to see," says the singer, just before intoning his song. Is what the ear hears really what we hear? Is what the eye sees really what we see? What the mirror reflects is just the apparent face of a hidden evil. The living fleeing from their ashes; the dead resting there. Two giant eyelids close again over a gigantic shadow. Only the child who kept the autumn of his childhood in his notebook still dreams like the bird that sustains itself on a wing. The child who looks for the angel of the night in the light of day. He looks into the eyes of domestic animals. He looks at them attentively for a long time and then leaves, running, laughing, and forgetting everything.

We saved the last day for the pyramids. We walked around them as if in a pagan procession. The steps of the camel on the sand created a rhythm similar to that of a heart nearing its last beats. I hear it say, "You have been absent for a long time. Where are You, You whose absence was prolonged?" I hear the sigh of the thirsty land when a cloud passes over it. I ask myself in turn: "Whose breathing is this? Yours or mine? And why have we agreed to choose the pyramid, the greatest pyramid, to bury at its feet the secret code of our union, while before us the sand adopts a new form with the wind of every storm?"

The Perfume Tree

The aroma at the beginning...

The aroma reaches you in its full splendor and invades you. It comes from a woman. Let's call her "the scented woman". Woman stabbed by perfume. It is from pain that an oyster and its wounds give birth to a pearl. And it is the woman's suffering that gives birth to perfume. She becomes a cathedral and a saint. A rain of petals falls on the morning dew, impregnating light itself. She finds shelter under the tree of perfume; she lies there, mysterious and confused. Unsteady. Fascinating, seducing, permanent. She is there for all the women who are already born and for those who are yet to be born. She is among us, but we don't know where she comes from. She is like the deep golden light on a Rembrandt canvas, like the gold resting on an icon.

We find shelter under the perfume tree. Outside the city, of course. The trees from the city are defeated since birth and live in pain. A tree, like a galloping horse, demands the vastness that belongs to itself and to the air. Wandering trees, unlike trees from the city, grow in places of high altitude, in the mountains, in the flatlands. It is only there, in the immensity of space, where an open crack above the sky and light exists. It is also above the first star shining in the darkest night, taking with it the secrets of the universe. It is there where we give in to the whims of the seasons. With our open eyelids, we see the emergence of the sprouts. We hear the murmur of the opening leaves as they acquire the shape they are destined to take. We hear the flapping of the wing that waves through the air. We look at the ray of sun passing through an absent-minded leaf, illuminating its inner soul. And, for an instant, we forget that time passes and we become eternal. We are eternity in that instant that is passing.

The smell at the beginning. The smell of crazy grass. Of air washed by the rain. Of milk on a nipple forgotten by a newborn's mouth. Viscous milk of light yellowish color. The smell of maternity. The smell of trees with fruits that are about to rot. The smell of late summer. The smell that comes from memory. The smell of abandoned churches and blown candles. The smell of nudity. One's own nudity, to be precise. That of a mixture of moss, seaweed, and sulfur. She leans against a branch of her own perfume. And her perfume is a mixture of jasmine, menstrual blood, and iodine. Who, then, is responsible for exploding the dormant alchemy inside her limbs?

She stays inside, in a cushioned place. It is there, particularly, where she enjoys meditation. She closes her eyes while reading the books that she always loved, the books about forests, seas, and cities, and she listens to Caccini's Ave Maria. She thinks the singer's voice is different from Callas' voice. Callas' voice is the true image of the gods' pain when they fall in love. Orpheus, who added two strings to his lyre, could seduce gods as well as humans, animals, and minerals. He could even seduce the gods of the underworld when he went there to get his beloved's life back. But when he realized that he had definitely lost her, he found himself alone and inconsolable. She says that Callas' voice is the daughter of Greek tragedy which she knows how to caress and whose deep mystery she understands. With respect to the voice of the other singer, it resembles the gold of icons that rise above dawn and dusk. The voice cries to the purity of this gold. Coming from a sacred place, it remains sheltered from the contradictions and ambiguities of the world, from hope and sorrow. Nevertheless, the two voices, in perfect symbiosis with the music, beyond the words being vocalized, are let out like elements of the earth strongly tightened toward the absolute: wind-mountain-clouds. This triangle crowns the sea and its waves.

She looks around in silence. She can feel her ideas spinning around her head, but she cannot manage to convey them clearly. Like the perfume of a rose, the precise expression is unspeakable. Just like a volcanic eruption. Or a mute and piercing pain. A word can only express what is visible; however, she knows that the most important thing is invisible. She also knows that a word cannot surpass itself, but is surpassed when used to build a bridge to connect to silence. A word is not considered an end. Endlessly, she asks, "Do you know what a woman's body looks like at the moment of ovulation?"

"How her baby is breastfed with perfume?

"Have you ever desired someone to the point of desiring even their damnation?

"This is the ladder I climb. I climb endlessly. You vanish. I offer you a handful of sand and I let you infiltrate quietly inside me. We become a desert. Is it possible to find a small vineyard and stay inside it, now that we have all this greenness in our hands?"

Bless you! Oh, hope!

What should we do, then, when we want to sleep, but the smell of our beloved does not sleep with us, and neither the taste of her animality, the sweet tone of her voice, and the softness of her tempting mouth?

Even here I could see her features in this painting that a painter from the fifteenth century had chosen as the most radiant representation of Mary. I could see her among the four intermingled hands: the woman's and the child's. It's here that the painting begins, and rises to meet the supremely refined and noble featured face. She is accompanied by two trees brought from distant gardens. One is at her right and the other is at her left. The mysterious perfume comes from gardens in paintings. Its beauty on canvas comes from the same beauty fixed somewhere in the carelessness of time.

Oh, sky of countless stars that are born and die, give me some of your apparent purity!

The End of Waiting

Having waited too long, there comes a moment when we no longer wait. The cloud passes over the desert to rain elsewhere. If what we have spent our entire lives waiting for comes unexpectedly, we won't be there to receive it. The thing we desire, counting the days until we have it, kept awake entire nights by it, holding onto it as the priority of all priorities, becomes, after time, a futile pursuit. Not only because the thing so desired did not come at the most opportune moment, but because the notion of opportunity itself is limited by time, which is capable of overcoming the strictest surveillance.

During my childhood and adolescence, that is, before my departure from that country as high as the sun, my mother used to wake me up in the middle of the night to make sure I was still alive. I would wake up suddenly to see her standing over me, or leaning against me, with her ear next to my chest. Seeing me awake, she would smile, surprised, and I was wary of that smile which betrayed her fear of death. It made my heart tremble. My mother's behavior led me to begin locking the door of my room before going to sleep. Since my room overlooked the garden, I would go in and out of the window like a thief. As I went in and out, I would inhale the fragrance of the jasmine and orange trees, which followed me beyond the low wall of the garden. Since then, my sleep has been restless. I wake up any time someone walks into my room, even if they are barefoot. Upon waking in the morning, I ask myself whether I spent the night asleep or awake. It has got to the point that I feel I can be woken up even by a noise as slight as a tree branch rustling inside the dream of the woman sleeping by my side.

Very possibly, the process of waiting unfolds within us as we dream.

In a dream, I see myself lying down on hot sand. Sand of an endless desert that stretches into infinity. I see you coming from far away, wearing a black two-piece bathing suit. Smiling, you hurry toward me. Your foot touches mine, but I stay still. Your smile gives way to another one, a bigger smile. It's not the forced smile that you flaunt in front of a mirror, or even in front of me sometimes, but a smile that comes from the bottom of your heart, completely spontaneous. It is the light of those things that have a secret to reveal. Light of a diamond, a pomegranate, a gardenia, that smiles at me when I surprise you in the darkness.

In the dream, you appear before me, shining with a strange and alluring radiance. Then, you suddenly approach me. You kneel high on my chest. I become the object of your contemplation. You smile again and I wonder what you see in me. I feel a little confused. In my dreams, I always try to gather all my strength and focus. Distracted for a moment, I say to myself, "How white she is!" I have told you many times about this fatal whiteness that can lead our eyes to see beyond the visible. A whiteness so powerful it can steal the sight from our eyes. But I don't think you have been listening. Your countenance remains the same. Turning toward me, you seem to be coming from far away. I don't move at all, but you keep approaching with the same smile. And then, from where you are, you rest the tips of your toes on my closed lips.

Sometimes dreams can condense beauty. With a condensed force, I feel your tongue and teeth illuminated by your smile. The image of your face and radiant mouth at the moment of ecstasy. And this energy, lively and invigorating, implodes in your body under the influence of your uncommon urges.

A woman is capable of revealing what is in her heart with audacity and beauty beyond compare. A woman possesses at once the secret of silence and the secret of words. A woman's voice keeps the secret of a rose. Her secret precedes her wherever she goes; her star accompanies her.

Our relationship lasted seven months. It lasted until she told me, looking at me with her eyes full of calm, "I think I am falling in love with someone else." Her voice was warm and tender when she uttered those words. That same voice which just the night before, as both of us lay naked on the bed, described the fuchsia color bordering a grayish blue cameo.

At first, it seemed to me that she was saying something that didn't concern me. Strange. I didn't react immediately. A sort of torpor, a kind of stillness spread through my body. I thought that her calm and soft voice was telling me, as usual, a charming story in which the hero looks for a way to escape with his beloved, once and for all.

How could I have known that what she was saying concerned me, when we were so close to each other? The sound of that breathing that took away my loneliness, wasn't that hers? Had she finally understood that it was better to abandon the floating raft, before it was too late?

Proximity does not mean stability or shelter. She is there before you, and you wait for her as you've never waited for anyone. Warmly. Burning. Immersed in waiting. Waiting for her to stay beside you, waiting for her to leave you, and even waiting to leave her. And when what has to happen finally happens, what is foreseen from the very beginning, you retreat to a meadow in your secret garden, looking everywhere to see if she's waiting for you.

Suddenly, we realize that there's no longer anything or anyone to wait for. That's how it is. We walk with someone to the end of the road, and then separate. At the beginning, like two survivors from a shipwreck, we hold on to the only floating plank in the water. We approach each other to avoid

drowning and loneliness, and then we forget. Oh, how light and soft oblivion is when it reaches us, like a delicate breeze that touches our foreheads and then disappears. Like two survivors from a shipwreck, united by the same fate, we save ourselves from drowning, and the sea becomes our ship and salvation. Then we forget. And when we wake up, time has already slipped away. Did Ulysses really wait for his return to Ithaca, to his wife and his dog? Wouldn't he have wished, after those long years of waiting, never to go back to his home? That country, dissolved in time, transformed into memory, is it still possible to recover it just as it used to be? Wouldn't it have changed completely? And those who waited for Ulysses, did they truly wait for him? Didn't his return make them feel uncomfortable? And who is it that returns twenty years later?

Did Noah really wait forty days and forty nights before leaving his ark? Wouldn't he have wished to stay inside, accompanied by his family and animals, sharing the air freely with them, far from the vastness that had separated them? After a long battle with illness, wouldn't Job, like Badr Chaker Assayyab, who came thousands of years after him, have wanted to exit the tunnel?

Did Assayyab really want to get well from his illness? Wouldn't he have preferred to return to that place where there was neither pain nor the illusion of waiting for what would never come?

We wait for everything except the return of the dead. Or maybe not. Even after death, we wait for a return. Didn't Martha wait for the return of Lazarus?

I have never really understood why Lazarus decided to return after his death, knowing that he was going to die again. No one would be there to hold his hand and save him the second time. I wonder if the acceptance of a temporary return to life was to please his sister or his Lord.

His resurrection, however, which was indeed more painful than his death, would never have happened if his sister hadn't wished for it. Without that wish, the Lord Himself wouldn't have defied the will of death. They both looked in the same direction, in complicity, and a strange, mysterious, and exciting sparkle appeared. It is still there, two thousand years later.

If this hadn't been the case, who would have woken him from his profound sleep? What would have prompted him to emerge from the womb of the earth and its infinite grace? How many years did he survive in his resurrected state? Did he regret it? But how did he manage to return to the land of the living? Under what pretext?

Two deaths and one life, such is Lazarus. The second time, the swallow of death was more decisive in the body, more penetrating. Martha was already dead. The woman who waited for his return the first time was no longer there. Who, then, would ask for his return after that? Every return presupposes a call. The call of someone who waits. If such were not the case, how and why would it happen? When there is no one waiting for our arrival and no one to see us off when we depart, how do we know it is time to leave?

Martha left and then the Lord left. People say that they were last seen together swimming in Lake Tiberius. After that, any trace of them vanished from earth. The story of crucifixion served to show the Son of Man as a being above all other men. To make him a scapegoat. The victim whose sacrifice raises him above those for whom he sacrificed himself. Beautiful is the sacrificed one, the wounded one, lifted above the mass of victims, he who found neither name nor attribute. Nothing else that needs continual sacrifice, to be the ideal victim, since Abraham. And from Abraham to the victims of the atomic bomb, which fused together the bodies of all the inhabitants of the afflicted city. It fused them into a giant corpse that spread itself as dust over the ruins of the world.

And after the wait is over, what happens? We wait for the end of wars. Then we wait for wars to start again. We wait for the end of disease and hunger. For the end of the rains. For the end of day, then of night. We wait for love. For the time of fertility. For the mystic blue of a Sufi night. We wait for beauty and for our guardian angel. We approach them as we would approach a precipice. Then there is nothing more to wait for. Nothing at all.

Even waiting dies.

Planet

The Earth is beautiful.

Beautiful is the cloud that travels by itself in the blue sky, like a bird that is lost and disoriented in its flight. The stars are also beautiful, and their unsteady lights are strange. They are the guardians of an infinite space. They watch you from a distance and know you, but you don't know them. Do they perhaps pity you because you ignore what is awaiting you beyond the threshold? Unless these stars are aware that your fate is also theirs.

Tender is the merciful breeze that touches the forehead in the distant summer of the islands. Tender is the rain moving agilely on the thirsty grass. Tender is the perfume of the unknown woman who walks beside you and continues along her way.

Our encounter was beautiful before it stumbled on the details. That encounter was like a crescent moon on which we hung our dreams.

Beautiful is the Earth when my soul leaves it. I contemplate it, like an astronaut from a window. I see its blueness, illuminated from the inside. It lifts its white veil and precedes me wherever I go.

Beautiful planet, our Earth, heading to its end with a strange delight.

- II -

Quiet

For the hungry in the cities, the distant wheat fields seem to extend beyond infinity, as if there were no hunger under the sun.

Do you know the hunger of the cities? The hunger of the labyrinth that leads to neither land nor tree. The greatest hunger of all. The hunger of the one who is absent even from himself.

I

I am Al-Hallâj, the unfortunate, the crucified. I bleed my thirst. Looking at my parents, I barely recognize them. And neither my friends wrapped in the good conscience of money. I don't recognize the wild animal that entered my daydream and woke me up. I don't know my name. I don't know the dust that conceived me and the dust that awaits me at the threshold. Between birth and death, there is a space that can't be named. An arc that doesn't throw arrows... On a paper, I draw the talisman of my soul and also the remains of my body spread here and there. My body doesn't belong to me as I don't belong to it. My body that runs to its destiny as I run to mine. Help me, oh, You who burn inside me, to find my destiny.

Help me, You, who's face I can't see but only its light. Free me from what moves me away from You and revives my desire for You. What I call and pronounce has no name. Looking at You, I see branches made of corals and a diamond taking shape. Morning flows as dawn is announced. With You, I find myself outside love and hatred. I am empty of life down here and empty of the afterlife. Outside the rotating earth. The space I live in is You. Nowhere else beyond You.

There is no body or place to contain me. And neither plain nor mountain. My blood flows out of my body and my body flows out of me. I can't stand any roof above my head and sometimes, in moments of ecstasy or absence, I say one thing and immediately say the opposite. However, nothing prevents me from telling the truth. I am the author of that which is attributed to me and that which is attributed to others. My passion increases as pain purifies me. And I have no fear. When I am carried to the cross and see wood and nails, I burst out laughing. Only the one who does not fear death does not fear crucifixion. Only the one capable of forgiving, beyond good or evil, is capable of confronting the universe.

A long wooden board crosses another of shorter length. Two pieces of wood of different lengths float in space. One for the hands, the other for the head and trunk. Here I am in the air, hoisted in this wooden boat, crucified. Floating there where the body cannot be distinguished from the spirit. Spread wide. Simple, light, as a feather. My cross, which has joints, makes me go up and down or down and up, and it makes me turn from left to right or from right to left, in all directions, sometimes quickly and sometimes slowly. It moves at a crazy speed before standing still like a bird resting in the air. My head is at the bottom of the log. From here I look at the sky. I sit near its blue extension while my wounds bleed like snowflakes. As I approach death, I feel a strange and rare pleasure that the living don't know, unless they are, like me, in this border that separates the two worlds, with a guide like mine. Help me, Oh Guide, to cross the border...

II

I am Rabi`a Al-Adawiyya. In this life, there is no one but Him who matters to me. He, the absolute one. Those who don't know me don't believe in me. I don't believe in myself. For Him I left everything, opening my arms to the Unfathomable. The only One. The Impeccable, the Irreproachable. The one with whom nothing can be compared. A burning desire pushes me toward Him. No, that is not desire, but something that resembles death. And what if He were death?

I am Rabi`a of Basra and not Rabia, Ishmael's daughter, with whom books have mistaken me. I came to this world in a hut deprived of even the most minimal ointment for a newborn's survival, the most minimal source of light, the most minimal piece of jute for the cold. My father prayed on his knees one hundred times. He did it four hundred times on Fridays. I was very small when he died. The bandit who bought me sold me for six dirhams. Thinking that my life would last only a few days, I decided to risk it. I stayed up most of the time, fearing that if I slept, I wouldn't wake up. Such was my suffering that anything looked beautiful and magnified inside my heart. For a moment, I would forget that my body was made of dust. Alone at night, I would hear the music coming from a distance, while the perfume of eternity filled my nose. I understood then that there was a secret inside me. I remained silent and listened. One night, in seclusion, as my body was writhing in pain and deprivation, I heard a voice telling me, "Don't be sad, at the Last Judgment in heaven, you'll be envied by others." At that moment I was certain that the light would inevitably come. Then I started to play the flute, glorifying the star of the day that breathes life into the soul of every living thing.

I carry fire in one hand and water in the other. He is my fire and my water. My remedy. Water for my body when it burns, and fire when my body is cold. His face is omnipresent. It fills me and consoles me. And when I cry, which happens very easily, He passes through me like a ray of light that passes through a gray cloud. I tremble with His shiver. He wants me to be His and I want Him to be mine. I call Him with all my strength, in silence:

"The more I desire You, the more my body shrinks. I get tongue twisted and that makes me say nonsense. Oh, release me from my five senses and set me free in Your vastness. Make me a grain in Your land, a cloud in Your sky, but don't deprive me of seeing Your face. I know that in order for You to show Your face, the blood of the entire world is needed down here."

I call You. Give me a little bit of time to be myself, to be what You would want me to be: deprived of everything except my desire for You. What can a drop of water contribute to an ocean of thirst? I am the drop of water and You are the ocean. You are the storm. You are the tear on my cheek and my foam. These golden bubbles shine when they see You. But You shine more than them. My eyes wander, looking everywhere, but You are always the image they see. You are my partner in this desolated road. Let me hold Your hand. Let me take Your skin and blood. Your sky and stars. Everything inside me is beautified for You. My heart, above all. It seems to drown as I can hear its forceful, long, and deep beating. So then, who can dare to say that we were not born together?

III

I am Francis, Francis of Assisi. I love the birds in the sky and pregnant women. I love full breasts and I don't need to eat in order to live. I call trees by their names and I guide birds to their nests. I talk to wolves and I am not afraid of their jaws. I love Clara. The beautiful and wonderful Clara who shaved her head and left her family for me. I love her because her lips only open to express amazement for the beginning of a new day, a river running on the pebbles, a branch that twists in the furious wind. She gathers the constant movement of the earth in the silence of her heart. Her way to sit under a cypress, at dusk, resembles the way she sits near her soul. Meanwhile, sitting under another cypress, I contemplate her.

An hour after the birds finished chirping, the trees slowly capsized in the darkness. Turning my eyes to the place where you were sitting, Clara, I couldn't see anything else. Turning my eyes to the sky, I saw the first shining star completely alone in this vast game field. I saw it twinkling, as if it were announcing the opening of a ball. At that moment, I didn't know my praying companions were watching me. They were watching my oily forehead, shiny in the light, and they saw me rise a few centimeters above the ground, and even up to three meters, as tall as a poplar. At times, they also saw me floating up in the sky, surrounded by a halo of light.

Apparently, it was enough for me to enter into a deep state of prayer or to watch Clara on her knees, about to pray to fly away. I wasn't aware of this because, immersed in a state of meditation and rapture, I couldn't see or hear anything. However, the day Clara suddenly died, I felt a strange happiness. She was, certainly, the dearest woman in my heart, but her presence had become so haunting that she often took control of my soul, even during prayer. She was so beautiful that I tried to avoid looking at her; her beauty startled me. She must have known that, as every woman who possesses the heart of a man does. She would sit under the same cypress and fade along with every dusk. She would fade, day after day, giving the impression that she was getting lost forever in the calm of the night. Oh, the night, fallen at random in this distant region of a period which was later known as the Middle Ages.

Shortly after her death, I had the feeling that I would die instantly if I didn't somehow use all the energy inside me. An energy that ran out, that wore me out due to my obsession with her. Did she leave this world because of me, because I was the reason for her well-being? On that day, I decided that nothing would distract me from the movement of living beings, large or small. Then, I started to plant in soil, working tenderly with my hands, and to feed hay to the donkey, who stayed under the sun for hours. However, the best thing I did before my departure was to remodel the church Notre Dame des-Oiseaux. In the mountain where I found shelter after forty days of fasting and praying, with my eyesight nearly lost, I began to see things I was not supposed to see. Paradise and hell in the same skylight. The living and the dead together. And with them, all of those who will be born. I saw myself flying high above the plains of beautiful Umbria and, during colorful sunsets, capturing an edge of the sky and taking it from its place, destroying the horizon and the border between sky and earth. Then I continued flying, wandering, flapping my wings, before stopping suddenly, staying motionless in the air, with my unfolded wings amid infinite space.

On the forty-third day, I found myself naked on the mountain, under a heavy rain. I was very thirsty. Facing the sky with my mouth open, I began to drink. I felt my whole body quenched. After some time, the rain stopped and the clouds dispersed giving way to a bright and mysterious light that blinded me. I opened my arms, imploring. And five powerful rays of light directed toward me pierced through my hands, feet, and waist before they disappeared with the bright and mysterious light. When I looked at my hands, feet, and waist, I noticed that they were bleeding. When the bleeding stopped, I saw stigmata similar to those left by the nails that pierced my Lord.

Experiencing the worst suffering was a way to alleviate His suffering from the centuries old crucifixion. When I woke up early the following morning, I realized that I was almost completely blind. Feeling my way in the space around me, I began to glorify the dawn, the sun about to rise, the generosity of nature and its animals: the wolf, the bird, the sheep, the fish. Since then, I have become the saint of all those who love nature. Much later, I learned that Giotto would tell my story and the events of my life in frescoes painted on the walls of the basilica in Assisi and that an earthquake would hit this seismic region and destroy not only the walls and frescoes of this house of God, but also entire herds grazing in the plains. It will happen some time before the Last Judgment.

Animals and minerals are my friends. What dark force pushed me to the abyss? I don't regret anything about my life, not even what I suffered against my will and the pain that I inflicted upon my father. I regret, however, one single thing: having preached proselytism to the Andalusian Arabs in Spain and even to the sultan in Egypt. Am I completely responsible for that? Isn't the period I was born into also responsible? A privileged period, indeed, for its sermoning and preaching.

IV

I am Teresa. Teresa of Avila. I love men who inspire insatiable desires in me. I love them but their water is scarce. I love them in Him, the Infinite and only One. The One who quenches my thirst without keeping count or drying up. I love writing letters and I only write to Him. I write with my whole body and with sweat on my forehead. With the burning fever of the night. I miss Him and I cry because of this deprivation which makes me burn. He is my lover, my husband.

Sometimes I am afraid of the Inquisition because I have said that to die is to enjoy Your presence. The butcher is before me as on a canvas by Velazquez or Goya betraying the tradition of the people. Oh, the horror of hell on earth for those who pretend to love You. I am afraid of the crowd that surrounds You on Palm Sunday and kneels before You, purifying themselves as they touch Your clothes, and on the following day, they hold Your cross with all of those who crucified You.

Everything is vain and ephemeral. I sleep very little and when I wake up, I am no longer what I was. An angel appeared before me holding an arrow that can throw lightning. Looking at me with shining eyes and a mysterious smile on his lips, he directed his arrow toward my heart and penetrated it several times, ripping up my entrails and leaving me out of breath as he removed the arrow from me.

Now the owner of my heart, the angel takes me to paradise. He is my remedy and consolation. His wound against my heart. The wound that provokes pangs of desire in me, after which there can be no sadness, no dissatisfaction. No one but Bernini knew how to express my joy. No one but him knew the degree of my pain and the height of my ecstasy, almost touching death. Today, I rest in the purity of his stone and the complexity of his marble, knowing that the beautiful angel is still looking at me even though I don't see him. Is there any way for me to belong somewhere?

I discovered the first signs of my path through stories of knights from mythical times and stories of my brother's trips on board one of the first ships that sailed the Atlantic toward the New World. Since the time for words has come, I choose one of those signs to tell you only one of those stories.

Three days before his departure, my brother had a strange dream. He was on board one of the ships that transported black slaves carried with thick iron chains. It was the first time in his life that he saw men and women of dark skin. They were gathered like pigs in the hold of the ship. Under the orders of a member of the crew, they were forced to dance in order to exercise their limbs numbed by entire days crowded in darkness. Those who disobeyed were whipped. The slaves, even chained to one another, danced. Faced with this, some women threw themselves into the ocean...

Continuing his tale, my brother said, "As the voyage lasted an eternity, we became exhausted. Meanwhile, in the hold, one by one, the slaves were dying from exhaustion and hunger. Every morning, bodies were thrown into the ocean. Only about half of this human cargo reached the destination with us. Only those who were able to resist the diseases, the hunger, and the exhaustion were fit to work on the land, in mines, and also in convents. The women and children were enlivened as we anchored at sunrise. They were naked. The children ran along the beach while the women, with babies in their arms, looked at us at a distance with astonishment and distrust. Then, all of a sudden, the women disappeared, giving way to a group of men, also naked, savage-like, and uncivilized. After the ship was firmly anchored, the first to descend were the missionaries carrying crosses. They planted the biggest cross on the soil, raised their hands to the sky, and turned to the open-mouthed men, asking them to pray to God, while the conquistadors tried to inquire about gold. Evidently, there was a big confusion."

Later, my brother learned that the shore on which the ship had landed, in his dream, was the coast of Mexico. It turned out that the native Mexicans had also dreamed that one day around that period of time, bearded men with a feathered snake on their heads, coming from behind the ocean, that is, from where the sun rises, would visit them. Cortes too dreamed of reaching that place one day, galloping on his horse. With his men, he climbed to the top of a temple and asked King Montezuma to renounce his gods. But the king, who was the spiritual leader of the most civilized nation of Central America at that time, could not contain his anger and said, "If I would have known that you would utter such offending words, I would never have allowed you to present yourself before my gods." When Cortes continued to humiliate the king, the latter replied, "What do you expect from me when I expect nothing else from life?"...

I, Teresa of Avila, realize now that I misinterpreted my brother's dream, as I wrongly took sides with the conquistadors, my compatriots. It is true that I was afraid for their lives and prayed for them throughout their long journey to the new continent because at that time, I considered them the saviors of souls. I, Teresa of Avila, from where I am today, I see immense forests of lush trees, innumerable rivers, currents of waterfalls and rocks, and I hear, with my heart in my throat, the echo of some words left by the native Indian: "The clean pine tree, the sandy river, the cloud over the dark forests, the illuminated skylight, and the buzzing of the insect. Everything is sacred in the memory of my people and in their hardship... When the last red man disappears from earth, his memory will live like the shadow of a cloud over a meadow. The souls of my Indian brothers will live forever in the river banks and forests because they and I love this land as much as an infant loves the beating of his mother's heart."

V

I am Simeon Stylites. I am a foreigner in this land and I wish I could climb it. I sleep little; I am awake most of the time. Yet, that is still insufficient for praying. From the height of my column I can see the sky as no telescope can show me. And I hear sighs coming from a distant world. Who says that the extraterrestrials haven't yet trampled on our earth? They have been here for a long time, but they have become invisible since they are much more advanced than us. They are here, around us, everywhere.

I am Simeon. I love astronomy. My dreams know no limits. I love the wind, the rain, and the seasons. The sun rotates around me seven times, to remind me that I am here temporarily and that my column, built in this place, will bear witness to that. Who am I to hinder the night from its secrets? To carry all these stars over my head? To accompany the movement of the breaking waves in my heart? To make the distance between sky and earth as evanescent as a spider web? Who am I to gather in a single heart all the states and contradictions, letting my soul wander freely like a lonely cloud fallen behind, as small as a grain of wheat?

Although illiterate and credulous, I was a strong and innocent shepherd. Like a wild goat, I used to run and jump on the Syrian plains, following my shadow everywhere it went and with my shadow, blowing in the wind. Escaping from poverty, I left my parents and found shelter in a convent. I would eat only once a week, while my mates ate every three days. The superior became furious when he learned about this. Such was his anger that he almost fainted. He hit me with a thick cane, accusing me of disturbing the general order, and I was sent to a dark dungeon resembling a prison cell. There, I found a thick rope made of palm straws that made my heart startle. I made a belt and tied myself strongly. After about ten days, a wound began to bleed. A fellow monk in the convent, the same who brought me a glass of water and a piece of dried bread every day, smelled the strange odor emanating from me. He approached me and touched the rope. He had blood on his fingers when he left. A few minutes later, I heard footsteps rapidly approaching my cell. The door opened violently and a dazzling light rushed in. I couldn't see anything but I heard the superior's voice, a loud and disturbing voice. He rushed toward me, hit me again, and then tried to forcefully remove my belt. He tried in vain since I tied the belt so strongly that it became part of me. These brutal acts, hence, caused a hemorrhage. The superior's anger increased tenfold and he started to punch and kick me, then he dragged me to the door and threw me outside as he ordered me with his thunderous voice not to show myself in that place ever again.

This time spent in the dungeon, which lasted nine days and nights, revealed to me my ability to tolerate hunger and thirst. I also realized that I am a son of light because the only thing that I lamented when I was imprisoned was the daylight. I tried to keep in my eyes the secret place where light came from. When I finally managed to stand up, my body was covered with dust. I started to wander, tired and hesitant. I walked for a long time, until the monastery was out of sight and suddenly I had the feeling that all of that was just a dream. As I continued walking, I found shelter in an empty hut. On the following morning, a passing convoy stopped as they heard me groaning. These noises, which I can restrain when I am awake, must have escaped during my sleep. They approached me and took me out of the burning cask, then they moistened my mouth with a wet cloth because I was completely dehydrated. Once I recovered my strength, I went to a hill where I built a column where I have lived continuously for thirty-seven years. I attached a three-foot wooden panel in the column, and I tied myself to it with ropes so that I wouldn't fall if my continuous fasting deprived me of all my strength. My hands were stretched to the sky so that I could stand during the night, upright in front of everyone. From then on, my life and death would be like no one's. I would be the only "astronaut martyr saint" in the history of humankind. From then on, it would be impossible to categorize me in any book or record.

One day, a passer-by saw me. I, escapee from the world. Astonished, he told his friends and family about me. They began to pour in, one after another, surprised in turn, they recounted what they saw to anyone they met. Some were shocked when they saw me and thought I was crazy. Others believed in me and came near me so that I would bless them. This happened every night and after the people were gone, I continued to build my column. As the number of people, some coming from distant towns, increased the height of the column increased too, reaching seventeen meters. This column protected me from the numerous people searching for salvation. They came to me to find a solution to their problems. There were tribes of enemies that fought fiercely face to face, and I was required to separate the stubborn ones, treating them like animals, screaming like a madman. I was also the target of sarcasm. Some mocked me in whatever position I was in, erect or in a meditative posture. Later, they built a shelter near me, then another over night. But this wasn't all. They even started to imitate me like monkeys, and they ended up converting the area into a park of columns. Nevertheless, mine was still the highest one. The flow of crowds did not stop; on the contrary, the crowd continued to grow as my reputation as miracle worker became known everywhere. I don't understand how a suffering man like me can heal others!

There is no hunger under the sun.

Do you know the hunger of the cities? The hunger of the labyrinth that leads to neither land nor tree? A poor breast gives poor milk. The traveler travels alone. Facing the sky, he screams, "Where are You and what did You do? Why did You desert me? You, who give fire to volcanoes, give me something to calm my thirst. Give me a single moment of quietness and let it be as big as the earth and the world!"

Acknowledgements

Mirages was first published in Arabic by Dar An Nahar, then published in French by José Corti. The author and translator are deeply grateful to Sinan Antoon, Patricia Duffy, Elizabeth Reddington and Lindsey Boldt for reading and commenting on the text.

About the Author & Translator

Issa Makhlouf was born in Lebanon and lives in Paris. He is the author of several books including *Letter to Two Sisters* (recipient of the Max Jacob prize), and *A City in the Sky*, both published by Editions José Corti in Paris.

Alicia F. Lam is a Venezuelan-born biologist currently residing in New York City.